GUSTAV VIGELAND

The Sculptor and his Works

BY

RAGNA STANG

TRANSLATED BY
ARDIS GROSJEAN

TANUM – NORLI
OSLO 1980

© RAGNA STANG 1965

FIFTH IMPRESSION 1980

LAYOUT BY KAI ØVRE

MOST OF THE PHOTOGRAPHS BY
TEIGENS FOTOATELIER

ISBN 82-518-0152-4

PRINTED IN NORWAY BY
DREYER AKSJESELSKAP, STAVANGER

TO THE READER

This unpretentious little book is about a great and many-faceted artist. Gustav Vigeland holds a unique position in the history of Norwegian art. No one has had the ideal working conditions Vigeland had in his mature years, yet few have known such difficult early years as those he experienced in Oslo of the eighteen-eighties and nineties. How did he bridge these two extremes? How was it possible to succeed so thoroughly in the very community which had felt not the slightest responsibility for him upon his arrival there — a young man possessed of the curious ambition to become a sculptor?

The controversy surrounding Gustav Vigeland, his art and the problems connected with it, has continued for a long time, and it has often been intolerant in nature.

I have had the rare privilege of being able to build upon Vigeland's own words, even in those cases involving his misgivings and his faith in himself as a creative artist. Consequently, I feel it was only right to let him speak as much as possible, and to reproduce the comments, vituperations and praise, of others.

I trust the wealth of pictures will enable the reader to make his own evaluations of Vigeland's art. It remains to be seen whether he will agree with Italy's great author Luigi Pirandello, who said: *"Truly, I left the studio of the sculptor Vigeland filled with admiration. I felt quite stunned by the amazing power of his great works of genius."*

Ragna Stang

CONTENTS

Vigeland is assuredly one of the greatest of living artists ... The race of great creators, fecund and prodigious, is not exhausted; it lives to-day in Gustav Vigeland.

Lawrence Binyon
in "The Studio," March 1924

CHILDHOOD AND YOUTH

There is no strong sculptural tradition in Norway. In the late nineteenth century conditions were such that aspiring to be a sculptor meant a struggle for bare existence. It meant want, hunger and poverty to such an extent that Gustav Vigeland almost gave up the fight. However, he had set himself high goals, he had courage and he had confidence in his own powers. It would all be needed if he were not to succumb as other talented artists had done before him.

However, when people began to take notice of the young man, prominent Norwegian authors set about celebrating him in enthusiastic articles and Bjørnstjerne Bjørnson himself gave him the support of all his august authority. He was quick to use that powerful and perilous word 'genius' — a term which had already been applied to Vigeland at twenty by the man who was then Norway's only professor of art history.

Nor did Vigeland disappoint the expectations kindled by that term. When a competition was held for a monument to the mathematician Abel, Vigeland submitted a model which disregarded all the specifications and all the sculptural con-

9

Vigeland in front of the Abel monument (clay) on August 8, 1904.

P. 11: Vigeland's studio, now the Vigeland Museum. Architect: Lorentz Ree.

ventions, fashioning instead an apotheosis to genius itself in its flight through space and time. There is little doubt that the confident 32-year old artist had himself in mind as much as the ailing scholar who had died so young.

Just as Abel was borne through time and space by the two genii in Vigeland's monument, so Vigeland proceeded through opposition and trials to that moment in 1921 when, as a mature man of 52, he put his signature to the most remarkable contract ever entered into by an artist and an official body. Vigeland was to give the city of Oslo the rights to all he had created and all he would subsequently create. In return the city would build him a studio large enough to permit him to bring into being all the works he carried within him.

He wanted no money at all. Vigeland could have been a rich man if he had wished to sell his works to the many collectors, wealthy persons and museum directors who besieged him. However, from the day he determined that all his works

10

were to remain together, his answer was no. To meet his few personal needs he accepted an occasional portrait, or sold a wood cut. All he desired was to convert his dreams into reality, and this he was enabled to do to an extent surpassed by few, if any, artists.

The city of Oslo built him his studio, large and spacious — the studio which later became his museum. It was provided with a plaster workshop, a stone-cutting workshop and a smithy, and Vigeland was given all the artisans he needed to execute his projects. Thus, all the practical difficulties a sculptor normally encounters were eliminated. Vigeland could devote himself entirely to his creative work, secure in the knowledge that municipal authorities would preserve everything he made.

This is how the extraordinary Vigeland Park came into being. This vast open-air museum was and is his principal work. Yet it must not be forgotten that Vigeland left a large

11

Vigeland's parents, with Gustav in the middle.
P. 13: Gustav Vigeland in his youth.

body of work in addition to and in part ante-dating the sculpture park. These other works can be seen in the Vigeland Museum — some in the form of studies and models, others full size. It was on these works that the city based its decision when, placing its confidence in the artist, it approved the contract in 1921.

Vigeland's early works are imaginatively conceived, and they are filled with the heat of passion, with tenderness and sensitivity. The young Vigeland had much he wished to tell his fellow beings: about life and death, about fear and anxiety, sorrow and suffering. Joy seldom found its way into his art. Nearly all the early works are in the minor key. Even when his subject was young love, each figure remained in its own separate world. The woman stares past the man, and he past her.

Vigeland grew up in a stern puritanical atmosphere which marked him for life for, as he himself put it, "My childhood is always with me." And yet, at a later stage his work grew

more harmonious, losing some of its impassioned vehemence. The act of creation was no longer a confession as it had been in the early years when he had seemed to be trying to get rid of something. "You cannot go on like this, Vigeland," Bjørnson had once said to the young man. "You are burning up inside."

And perhaps he was. He was so filled with what he had to say that he did not always stop to consider the problem of form. This is dangerous for any artist, but all the more for a sculptor, form as an independent value being more important in sculpture than in any other medium.

Let us first take a closer look at the milieu he came from and the works he created in the difficult youthful years before the idea of the Fountain took possession of him.

Adolf Gustav Vigeland was born in Norway's southernmost town, Mandal, in 1869. His father was a carpenter and came of a coastal family. Vigeland has described the men on his father's side as violent and irascible. "They were like black storm birds who lived out on the rocks where the storms and the waves raged. They had long, narrow faces." His maternal grandfather however, was gentle and quiet and had an unrivalled talent for wood-carving. Vigeland's home was not a happy one. His writings tell of his father's moody and unbalanced personality. He has recorded how his father once tore the covers off himself and his brother Theodor and beat them — not because the boys were guilty of anything, but because it was Good Friday and one was supposed to suffer on that day. He never forgot such childhood experiences. They marked him and induced mental conflicts which may be the explanation for much of his later development. He related that his father occasionally drank too much, and that in remorse and contrition he would take the boys along with him to revival meetings.

Vigeland spent as much of his childhood on his maternal grandfather's farm as he spent with his own family in Mandal, and the reserved child was greatly attached to his mother and to her father. Gustav went to school in Mandal and to a rural school near his grandfather's farm.

In 1884 he was sent to Oslo to be trained as a professional woodcarver. His own wish was to become a sculptor, but when his father died in 1886, he had to go back home for two years to help support the family. When he was finally able to return to Oslo, he experienced extremely difficult times, of which he wrote several years later:

I came to Kristiania (as Oslo was then called) to become a sculptor. I wandered through the streets waiting for someone to discover me, to fish me out of the swarm as a genius. I had so often read things like that. But nobody came .... I walked and walked; I always looked profound; I strained my face and set my mouth like the pictures I had seen of great men. But nobody noticed me. I went on like that for many days. But

14

Wood-carving done in childhood. Self-portrait as a boy.

it couldn't last, of course. My money trickled away. Soon there was little, then nothing left. I went around for two days without an øre, but I would not look for work. I refused to be a wood-carver again; I clenched my fists. I wouldn't, not for the whole world. After all, I was practically a sculptor. For a long time now I had sat at home drawing and drawing, doing sketches for sculptures, for groups with motifs from Greek mythology and the Bible, for long reliefs with several hundred figures. And all that time I felt almost like a sculptor; all the time I was drawing I hardly touched a single wood-carving tool; they lay there rusting.

The boy had dreams of greatness, but it was not always easy to keep his dreams alive.

I lived everywhere and nowhere, in attics and cellars, and eventually I had to eat what was not really food ... I had a German translation of Horace, "Oden und Epoden," which I had had bound in thick cardboard. I took off the cover and soaked it in water so it swelled up. I don't know what was in it;

15

it must have been paste — flour paste — and it was by no means the worst thing I have tasted. The inside of the book I sold to a secondhand book-shop for 20 øre.

One evening I found a place in an attic passageway, but somebody must have heard me, because the whole family came up and stood on the stairs while a man shouted for me to come out. The maid came over to me, put her face close to mine and said, "No, he isn't drunk." Another time I was in an attic and was awakened by a woman stepping on me. She shrieked with panic and ran down the stairs screaming that there was a boy in the attic. People came out with lamps and I had to go past them. "He must be ill," a woman said; but they were a little afraid of me all the same.

I refused to write home.

I needn't say that I had pawned everything I could, and that I had nothing of value left. My overcoat was pawned, and a waistcoat, and my watch "Pancake." My dagger and I parted company right after Christmas. And no second-hand book dealer would take my books. I started to feel light-headed, dizzy and listless. One night I awoke and found myself outside town and freezing cold, calf-deep in snow. Then I really got frightened. I jumped up and began hopping and dancing like a madman to get warm again. I flailed myself with my arms, rubbed myself and in the dark my hands hit against the tree trunks. I'll never make it, I said to myself, I'll never make it. If I get back to town alive I'll go straight to the room I once had, fetch my drawings and go to Bergslien, the sculptor.

On reading this description of Vigeland's early youth one is reminded of another young man who came to Kristiania (Oslo) a few years later. Pedersen was his name, but he became the Nobel-prize-winner, Knut Hamsun. His experiences in "the city with the big heart," as Oslo sometimes styles itself, were similar, and he recorded them in a book which appeared in Copenhagen in 1890 bearing the simple title, "Hunger." It begins:

16

Knut Hamsun, dated April 17, 1903.

It was during the time I wandered about and starved in Kristiania; Kristiania: singular city, from which no man departs without carrying away the traces of his sojourn there. Both Knut Pedersen and Gustav Thorsen, as Hamsun and Vigeland were then called after their fathers, carried the traces with them.

The meeting with Brynjulf Bergslien was a turning point, and Vigeland has left a record of the encounter:

The following day (early in February 1889), *realizing that things could not go on as they were, I went straight to my former landlady, rang the bell and said that I would soon pay her what I owed and asked if I could get the drawings which were in my suitcase. She was friendly and said, "Go right ahead, go right ahead." I took them, forcing myself not to look at them, and went direct to Bergslien.*

The day was slushy as I went across the Youngstorv market-place where they were setting up the stalls. I walked in the direction of St. John's church to the place where Bergslien had his studio. I went round and rang at the back door; a girl with a fiery red face and round cheeks opened the door. I asked if Bergslien was in and said I would like to show him some drawings. She asked for my name; I told her and waited while she went inside. The porch where I was standing was rickety and the bell cord was plain string. The girl came back and said "Go right in," and I went down an old hallway where the floorboards were hilly and creaked at every step I took. I knocked on the door she showed me and heard a "come in" that seemed to come from under the ground. The studio was much lower than the hallway, several steps below it, and down there was fat little grey Bergslien with a red skull-cap, a long-stemmed pipe and a lorgnette, in the half-dark studio with its masses of dusty works, mostly busts, on shelves one above the other. It was warm there, and I was given a chair near the stove, and sat there while Bergslien thumbed through

Professor Lorentz Dietrichson (no. II, 1904) was among those who aided the young Vigeland.

the drawings. I noticed that he was working on a pair of reliefs with pictorial backgrounds. He leafed and leafed, and I hoped he would go on so I could warm myself still longer. "Did you do these drawings?" he asked without looking at me. "Yes," I answered, and I distinctly heard that s o m e o n e had answered yes. "Well I'll be damned if these aren't the best things I have seen. And you want to be a sculptor?" I don't remember what I answered; I didn't hear that I answered yes, but I must have. Then Bergslien said that he would talk to the professor of art history. "And then," he said, "I'll get some rich man interested. If the king were in town, I would go to him." And he asked if I would mind his keeping the drawings for a few days. "Of course not." "What is your address?" I gave him an old address, because I was afraid that he would not have anything more to do with me if I said I had no address and did not live anywhere.

I managed to arrange things so that I should come back on Thursday; this was a Monday. The days flew so quickly I hardly noticed. Thursday came, and I went to Bergslien who said, "It is all settled. You can begin here for the time being.

"Priam before Achilles." Drawing in the style of Thorvaldsen,
dated April 1, 1889.

*And now I am going to go out to the corner here with you and
rent you a room."*

*When Berglien saw that I could not take the change of diet
he sent me to a doctor who said I should live on milk and white
bread for a while. So there I was, modelling a relief on a theme
from Homer in Bergslien's studio two hours a day while he
took his afternoon nap. The rest of the time I spent at the
hotel, modelling a standing figure of a boy. Bergslien never
said that I ought to have a model to work from for either of
these projects.*

Bergslien showed the drawings to the professor of art
history, Lorentz Dietrichson. This is what Dietrichson wrote
five years later in connection with Vigeland's exhibition:

*One day in March 1889 Brynjulf Bergslien, the sculptor,
brought me a not inconsiderable sheaf of drawings by a young
man who was then 18 years old (actually, Vigeland was almost
20), who had come here from his home near Mandal in search*

Bertel Thorvaldsen: "Priam begging Achilles for Hector's body," 1815.

of instruction, intending to become a sculptor. Bergslien spoke in very strong terms of the astonishment he experienced at seeing all the drawings the young man had produced in his presence during the preceding days.

I am so used to seeing bright hopes fade upon closer examination that even though these words were spoken by a mature and experienced artist like Bergslien, I began to look through the drawings with misgivings. However, my amazement grew with each succeeding page. These drawings were dated, and the dates showed that in the month the young man had been in Kristiania he had gone far beyond Apelles' famous dictum, nulla dies sine linea, for here there was not merely a line for each day, but entire compositions, most of them designed for reliefs, and in such numbers that he must have averaged four or five per day. There were compositions with Biblical themes, motifs from the Iliad and other classical and more modern works, scenes from historical events and scenes from daily

21

life — all in changing, variegated profusion, all of them pro-
ducts of an imagination which was as rich as it was effervescent.
It was obvious that whenever the artist read a vivid passage he
pictured it living before his eyes, and needed only to set down
what he saw, just as others make notes on what they read.

It must be noted however, that these rich and varied compo-
sitions were by no means masterpieces. There was a general
weakness in the treatment of form, and there was a clinging
to certain ways of representing the human body which were
almost manneristic; yet there was an originality about it all
which, combined with the above-mentioned traits, for a
moment left me thoroughly perplexed ... I remember to this
day my first exclamation, "But this young man is in danger
of becoming a mannerist before he becomes an artist!"

Some of these drawings are still extant, and looking at them
one understands what Dietrichson meant. They are done in a
curiously impersonal, almost classical style. Young Gustav
Thorsen, as he was then called, had clearly taught himself to
draw in the manner of the earlier Danish sculptor, Thorvaldsen.
He had not copied him slavishly, but he had evidently come
across some drawing manuals of that period and had studied
them eagerly. It can also be seen that soon after his meeting
with Bergslien he abandoned this manner and found his own
personal style.

Dietrichson went on to describe the powerful impression
these early drawings made on him.

I remember exclaiming, thunder-struck, as I put down the
last sheet, "But here is a genius!" That is a word I use very
sparingly, but here I felt it was justified.

Bergslien spoke to some wealthy men in Oslo, persuading
each of them to donate five kroner (five shillings) a month
to his protégé. Thus began a new life for the twenty-year old
Vigeland. He had to make the rounds to collect the money in
person, and it was doubtless an errand that went against the

Studio of Brynjulf Bergslien, the sculptor.

grain of the proud and self-assured young man. Some years later he wrote in his notebook, "The services other people render me weigh me down like lead; I can never finish paying them off."

Vigeland studied with Bergslien for one year and attended classes at the School of Drawing in the evenings. Then one day Bergslien said, "Go to Skeibrok; he is the big fish among the sculptors here in town," and Vigeland went. While with Skeibrok he helped, among other things, to design one of the figures for the tympanum of Oslo University's main building.

"Satan," a drawing for the central figure in the relief Hell.

VIGELAND AND THE NINETIES

In 1889 Vigeland exhibited a small group, *Hagar and Ishmael,* at the annual State Art Exhibition. He was awarded a small stipend, and at the beginning of 1891 he travelled to Copenhagen carrying a letter of introduction from Professor Dietrichson to the sculptor, Professor C. V. Bissen. Here at last he found a congenial environment, and he also found a good teacher. He made friends too, one of which was the Danish sculptor, Brandstrup. Vigeland worked under Bissen for one year. It was in the tradition-steeped studios of the Danish Academy that his large group *The Accursed* came into being. This work attracted a good deal of attention at that year's official Danish exhibition, receiving much praise, and considerable criticism as well. In this work a characteristic can already be seen which was to become typical of Vigeland's entire production — his concern for that which is universally human — in this case, man fleeing from the awareness of his own guilt. The group lacks unity however, as the starkly realistic male figure does not quite harmonize with the more classically conceived female figure (p. 31).

Returning to Oslo in February of 1892, Vigeland found himself a small studio. He did not stay long however, for that autumn he went abroad again with another state stipend, this time to Paris — to the city of Auguste Rodin.

Vigeland never liked to hear anyone mention Rodin's influence on him, yet there is no ignoring it. It is true that he never actually became a student of Rodin's, but he did visit his studio several times.

Alone and penniless, the 24-year old Vigeland wandered about in the French metropolis. It was at this time that he wrote:

How easy it would be to make 'just a few' things which somebody or other would buy — dash off something allegorical, a compliment to men of commerce, for instance.

In a moment I would be on my feet; have heaps of money so I could begin on something for myself. But money is money! Perhaps I would gradually begin to bow and scrape, be assimilated by the moneymakers and become a philistine ... And t h a t is what I am frightened of, more than anything else. Oh, God, what am I going to do.

I have grown a little nervous lately. And what is the reason? Have I been drinking too much? No. Have I been carousing? No. What it all comes down to is money — too little of it. I have been observing others who are loaded down with these metal discs, these admission tickets, and seen that in relation to their abilities they do not deserve them ... And here am I, going around without money, devoid of these admission tickets to 'joy.' Not that I think my abilities are so great that they should be rewarded — not at all. I am a very average fellow, with average gifts. That is something I have come to realize. I am a poor artist, not much of a human being, not what you would call a comrade, and I am a mediocre friend ....

David, 1890.
Hagar and Ishmael,
exhibited at the
annual State Art
Exhibition, 1890.
P. 27: Hell II, 1897.

I am no good at modelling. I still lack technical skill. Nor is my approach to the human form valid. My figures lack consistency of character, they are only half-finished, and I am afraid I may start to develop mannerisms .. ..

In the summer of 1893 Vigeland was back in Oslo again, where he modelled his large relief, *Hell*. His intention was to make a series of four reliefs, among them *Paradise,* but he found he was unable to realize his plan. "No," said the young man who came from Norway's stern Bible Belt, "Paradise is something that is beyond my imagination."

In the autumn of 1894 he held his first one-man show in Oslo. It was given a mixed reception. One critic saw only horrors in the fifty works exhibited, while the art critic of another paper had this to say:

This is Vigeland's response to life, expressed in a uniquely personal art. It is pessimistic, if one is concerned only with

exteriors. But genius has baptized it by fire, making it an art of the life force, a flaming challenge to teach men how to live.

The young art historian, Jens Thiis, was also one of those who realized immediately that here was a new and promising talent, though he surmised, even at this early date, what was to be Vigeland's artistic weakness. *"This art is profoundly modern in the sense that it is a true product of its times ... As for Vigeland's formal qualities, they are rarely the best part of his art. His sense of beauty has not yet reached its full development. One searches in vain, in Vigeland's work, for the thoughtful, lingering treatment of each individual form which endows a work with the limpid and harmonious beauty which we term 'classical.' ... H e l l belongs undoubtedly to that category of works which an artist experiences as a tremendous personal liberation. It is as though all those bitter and painful impressions and all that sin and misfortune and suffering had rushed to meet him, had accumulated in his imagination and solidified in this gripping image. It will speak for itself, it will move everyone, and be understood by everyone.*

Consolation, 1893.
Shown at Vigeland's
first independent
exhibition in 1894.
P. 29: A drawing for
Hell.

On Vigeland as a portrait artist he writes: *None of our
younger artists are as adept at grasping what is essential in a
personality as he is.* As for Vigeland's form, he says that *it is
handicapped by a noble fear of lapsing into dullness. Not
infrequently this fear forces his striving for sharpness of form
into an angular leanness which occasionally threatens to become
a mannerism... I feel that the richness of his imaginative
powers justifies our greatest expectations, and in my opinion it
is our duty to safeguard this talented young man and his
masterpieces for our country.*

Vigeland's very first works were expressed in a style we can
best describe as classicist, such as the reliefs based on subjects
from the Iliad which he made in Bergslien's studio, or the group
Hagar and Ishmael, which is a fairly conventional little work.

His chief work from the Copenhagen year (1891—92),
The Accursed, shows us that in spite of the strong impression

the Danish sculptor Thorvaldsen had made on him, Vigeland
had by then broken away from 'classicising.'

Although Vigeland had already made a preliminary study
for *The Accursed* before he went to Copenhagen, his returning
to this motif, and his execution of this large group in the
biting naturalism of the day were certainly related to the
fact that a number of young Danes were then working in the
spirit of literary naturalism. Revealingly enough, this work was
originally called "Cain," and depicted the first murderer's
agonising qualms and his desperate attempt to flee from his
crime. The woman with a child on her arm and the uncompre-
hending boy accompany him on his flight. When the work
was first exhibited it aroused so much interest that the 22-year
old sculptor was jokingly called "the little Norwegian with
the big group."

The Accursed commands our respect. There are some
supremely achieved details such as the man's legs, arms and
shoulders. Nevertheless, there is something strangely theatrical

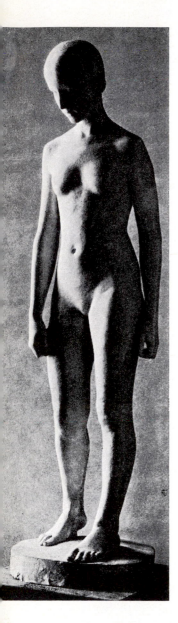

Young girl, 1892.
P. 31: The Accursed, 1891.

about the whole group that is characteristic of the period. Then too, as noted above, there is little connexion between the extremely naturalistic execution of the male figure and the more classically conceived female figure. In spite of Vigeland's intense study of live models and the resulting brutal naturalism, there is a certain externalism about this main work of the early years. In Vigeland's mature works this theatrical quality is not met with. Nevertheless, this group, with its universally human content, was a forerunner of the deeply felt portrayals of the soul which were to come.

Following the sojourn in Paris, where Rodin's art had made an indelible impression on him, Vigeland did a number of smaller works. They were reliefs mostly, some of them very shallowly worked, in which Vigeland employed a sketchy, evocative approach to tell of sin, judgment and death. There is the woman Rizpah sitting shrouded in her mantle, sorrowing over the hanging of her seven sons. There is Christ the Judge. There is the horse of Hell, trampling poor souls under its hoofs. There is the drunkard who plummets howling into perdition. Again and again Vigeland returned to these themes. A chilling air emanates from these delineations of sin and desperation, of judgment and punishment. Then he compounded all these elements into a kind of synthesis — the large relief *Hell*. The idea had long been smouldering in his mind, yet it is no mere accident that only after his stay in Paris did it begin to take definite form. There can be little doubt that in Paris Vigeland had stood enthralled before *La porte d'Enfer* (The

Gate of Hell), the masterpiece which had occupied Rodin since 1880.

It was typical of Vigeland that on Christmas Eve 1893, of all days, he began the first draught of this mighty relief depicting all the torments of life. For months he worked intensely until the first version was completed in 1894. He included it in his one-man exhibition in October of the same year.

However, this version did not satisfy him. In 1896, during his stay in Florence, he wrote in his notebook: *I want to do Hell over again, rework it completely. It may be good as it is, but it is not good enough.* Vigeland completed a new version in 1897, and it was then purchased by Norway's National Gallery. Subsequently he wrote to Professor Dietrichson: *Even more than the Renaissance works I had studied so eagerly in Florence, the ancient bronzes in Naples so revised my approach to form that it was imperative for me to go back and rework Hell from the very beginning.*

An examination of the first version of *Hell* reveals that its formal qualities are not its strongest points. It is as though this shattering narrative of perversity, perdition and damnation had overpowered him. The content is so dominant that the question of form is neglected. In his striving to depict terror and horror Vigeland concentrated on the facial expressions to the extent of over-emphasizing the heads, making them grotesquely large.

The final version, which is now in the National Gallery in Oslo, displays quieter rhythms. The composition centres upon Satan who sits enthroned, brooding over his kingdom. To the left, the gallows with its dangling victims terminates the composition. In the low relief of the background people float by as in a dream, while in the foreground the figures falling down in despair are modelled in a high relief approaching sculpture in the round.

The Resurrection, the companion relief to *Hell,* was never cast in bronze. There is no unifying composition here, only

Three merry friends at the photographer's in Trondheim, end of the 1890's.
Jens Thiis, Gustav Vigeland, Gabriel Kielland. Mask of the Polish poet
Stanislaw Przybyszewski. 1894.

people floating upwards, dreamlike, with eyes closed. In this
resurrection there is no rejoicing. Like silent shadows the
figures glide past. One feels that this relief could easily be
continued in all directions, for here there is neither beginning
nor end. This absence of a unified composition is certainly
deliberate, as the artist wished to evoke that which is timeless
and eternal.

By Vigeland's own account, *The Resurrection* was responsible
for an interesting discovery. One day many years after the
completion of the relief, he was carrying a photograph of it
which he had rolled into a tube with the picture side outermost.
The roll having shifted position, Vigeland noticed that it grew
slightly narrower at the top, and thus the idea occurred to

33

Man and woman. Drawing in
Florence on February 12, 1896.
P. 35: A poet. Drawing 1897.

him to recreate his earlier two-dimensional work, this time
doing it in the round. Thus the idea of the Monolith was
conceived!

One of those who were fairly intimate with Vigeland in
the eighteen-nineties was the Polish poet Przybyszewski, the
husband of Dagny Juell, a fascinating Norwegian girl. Vigeland
portrayed Przybyszewski in an interesting little bronze mask from
1894. It was in Berlin of the eighteen-nineties that a group of
artists and writers was formed, meeting as a rule in the wein-
stube "Zum schwarzen Ferkel". While in Berlin, Vigeland lived
in the same hotel as Edvard Munch, and in 1895 he did a bust
of this artist who was to become Norway's most famous painter.
Vigeland's friend Jens Thiis, whom he had already sculpted the
previous year, moved in this circle too. Vigeland also did a

portrait of Przybyszewski's wife, Dagny Juell, with whom the whole group was more or less in love. However, he destroyed the bust of Munch (it was rather a stormy friendship), and that of Dagny Juell as well. Strindberg, the Swedish dramatist, was also a member of the group. The drinking and merry-making were evidently intense, for in 1896 Vigeland noted: *As to whether or not Przybyszewski ever discussed my work thoroughly with me — well, it's hard to say. But from what I can remember of the Berlin days, I never spoke about my work; we only drank, the pair of us. I cannot even recall that we ever sat together and talked deeply about things when we were sober, no, that I do not remember.*

There can be no doubt that the Polish poet was greatly attracted by Vigeland's art however, for in 1895 he wrote a little volume called "Auf den Wegen der Seele" (On the Paths of the Soul). This book, which was published two years later, was dedicated to Vigeland. The author writes: *I shall speak of one of the chosen ones, one to whom the soul opened itself and revealed unutterable mysteries. He is the sculptor, Gustav Vigeland.* Whereupon follows a rather exalted description of Vigeland's art, written in the style which was typical of the period.

Przybyszewski found great significance in the fact that Vigeland was from Norway, "das tragischste Land von Europa." The book was actually written in Norway, and bears the date, November 1895. It contains sombre descriptions of Norway's scenery, of the Norwegian character and of the country in general, *this land of terrifying earnestness and harsh, heavy melancholy... Under the pouring rain and the leaden fog of the sky... a sky which even indoors lies heavy on one's head while evil, dismal thoughts bubble up as from a swamp... the naked and heretofore unknown life of the soul becomes possessed of unlimited power.* For a score or more pages he goes on to describe these morbid surroundings, showing how the young Vigeland had produced his early works in "this atmosphere of doubt and despair, in this hardened, desperate willing of all that is evil and in this brooding disintegration." He tells how Vigeland's entire artistic oeuvre is rooted in this anxiety-racked despair of the soul, and how the heavy, leaden sky and Jehovah's vengeful wrath weigh down upon all the works Vigeland has created. He finds the sombre, brooding eyes of the pessimist staring out of each work, the eyes of one "who is not capable of seeing anything in life other than suffering and brutality." At this point he proceeds to give a description of *The Accursed.*

Although Przybyszewski has a tendency to exaggerate, he does touch on something central and essential in Vigeland's art. A wave of deep pessimism did surge through everything he created in this period. All his motifs were taken from the same thematic area. He depicted doubt, anguish, sin and its corollary, "the wages of sin is death." As noted above, Vigeland once

wrote, "My childhood is always with me." In his notebook he recalled how his home in Mandal was a gathering-place for "fundamentalists, ministers, evangelists and 'brethren,' but never 'sisters.' There stern pietism held sway and his father grew ever more severe. Here is an account of the whipping in Vigeland's own words: *On the morning of Good Friday he (my father) came in to me and Theodor while we were still in bed, threw the eiderdown off us and raised Borka's (our horse's) whip above us. He did it because Jesus was lashed. It occurred only that once.*

It was such childhood experiences as these which marked Vigeland. All his early works illustrate themes chosen from life's darker side. It is as though with each work he were shedding something. He had to speak of all these things, not only because he wanted to communicate them to his fellow beings, but because for his own sake he had to speak out, to free himself from a sensation of doom by depicting damnation and the damned. Characteristically enough, it was the Old Testament and Dante's Divine Comedy which obsessed him in his earlier years. He never really outgrew this pessimistic attitude even

37

though his sombre melancholy gradually gave way to a mood that was gentler, if still in the minor key. In his later years a lighter, brighter tone could be detected, yet the drawings, letters and private journals of that time show his deep-seated distrust of people. Where women were concerned he demonstrated an almost unrelieved misogyny, and yet in his art he portrayed human love of the tenderest and most sensitive sort.

It was probably during the Berlin days that this attitude towards women crystallized, but the foundations were no doubt laid during the artist's childhood. Much later (in 1939) he wrote, "When I was little I often heard it said that women were not human beings." Antifeminine entries abound in Vigeland's notebooks, as for instance this one from 1900: *How ludicrous Ibsen is when he speaks of killing a woman's love-life! As though a woman's 'love-life' could ever be killed. But a man's can be killed! Write about that!*

Przybyszewski's conception of woman as a demonic creature was based on the premise that woman is the root of all evil. This view, which also influenced Edvard Munch, is clearly expounded in the little book which the Pole devoted to Vigeland. Few writers typified as he did the values dominant in the circles of artists and writers of the time, whether they were in Berlin, Paris or Oslo. Przybyszewski writes of woman's satanic influence through the ages, beginning with ancient times "when women were detested and despised." Then he shows how Christ "redeemed her and explained her evil nature," and how the Church in the middle ages considered her to be "worse than Satan himself." Whereupon, he claimed, there followed centuries displaying a fierce hate of women, excepting *the ridiculous eroticism of a few troubadours. Having relations with women meant that a man must sacrifice his immortality, it meant ruin in filth and shame. In the 17th century woman spread her venereal poison throughout the whole world: at Versailles, in the Vatican, in the monasteries and at the courts. Her power flamed up for one last time during the French*

38

Man and woman. 1906.

Revolution, then went into hiding in subterranean channels. Now our age sees woman in a new role, her cult of Satan modernized ... Munch and Vigeland synthesize the modern germanic woman, the woman who, though lacking the ritual traditions of the cult of Satan, nonetheless has the power of evil and the urge towards all that is evil dwelling within her.

This is truly a savage attack. And yet, however outlandish and even comical a book like "On the Paths of the Soul" may seem today, we must acknowledge that it provides a characteristic instance of the ideas reigning in the author's circle on art, women, life and death. Munch, the doctor's son from Oslo, was far more deeply affected by these notions than was Vigeland, the farmer's son from the South.

All in all, however, Vigeland did not feel particularly at home in this hyperintellectual milieu. After only three months he packed up and went to Florence. The following year he

P. 40: "The Oppressed" 1898.
This page:
Man and woman, drawn in Paris on Christmas Day, 1900.

made this note: "We seldom talked about that curious animal which the poets calls woman."

Przybyszewski ends his little book on Vigeland thus: *And his art is not popular art for the masses, nor is it an art for sickly, blasé nerves, for frail young men in perfumed rooms. It is the forever old, endlessly new art of the individual for the individual.*

In spite of the influence which was exerted by the nineties' view of woman as a demonic being, Vigeland's sensitive and withdrawn spirit did not allow itself to be shackled, and he enriched Norwegian sculpture with some of its finest portrayals of that ever new theme — man and woman. His works set before us ecstatic transport, devotion, melancholy and agony. They show us contentment, but rarely joy. In spite of everything his figures remain isolated in their own separate worlds.

Orpheus and
Eurydice, 1899.
The Hermit,
1898.
P. 43: Father
and Daughter,
1906.

In the lovely marble group from 1906 the two bodies are intertwined like the stems of young plants, but the man and woman do not look at each other. Each gazes thoughtfully past the other.

The group *Man Holding a Woman in His Arms* gives evidence of this same melancholy. The man bends tenderly over the woman, his eyes seeking her hidden face, as she lies there curled up in his strong arms (p. 165).

In a number of smaller groups from the nineties and the beginning of the century, similar attitudes are expressed. The group with the classic title *Orpheus and Euridyce* tells in wholly human terms of a man who tries desperately to hold a woman back, while she slips relentlessly over the edge of the precipice. In *Consolation* (1893) a young woman kneels comfortingly before an old man crushed by despair. An exquisite little study from 1898 shows a man tenderly pressing his head against a woman's groin. The same motif reappears somewhat altered in a large group dating from 1908 (p. 161 and 162).

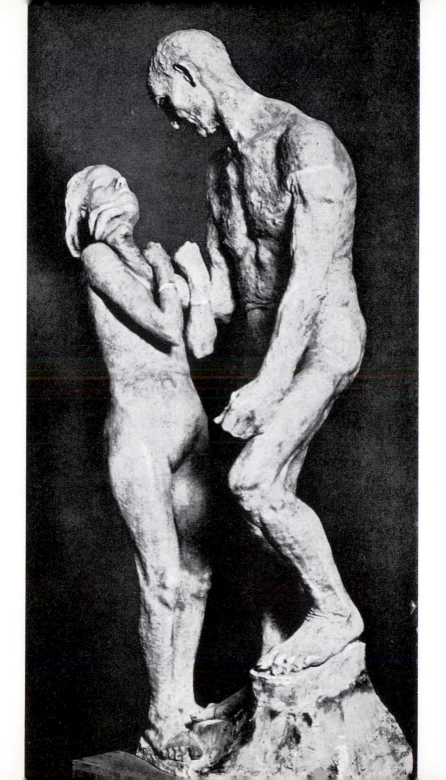

Vigeland appeared at the right moment. Norway then had certain writers and poets of international repute, she had a few talented painters, she had Edvard Grieg, but she had no sculptor of any stature before Vigeland appeared and took his place as a matter of course among the others, remaining there until his death. He had so much within him begging for expression. In his impassioned youth he demanded the utmost of himself. He wanted his work to embody all the human emotions, and thus the young Vigeland's psychological characterizations are truer, more revealing and more intense than those of any other Norwegian sculptor. The times demanded an emotional approach, in literature as well as in art. It has been said that Vigeland's early work was in the nature of a confession. Several of these works are so deeply personal that they are clearly stages not only in his artistic development, but also in his personal life. He seems to have rid himself of something with each of his works. It is this personal involvement which gives to his works their deeply human value.

However, it is just this which may be the root of his artistic weakness. For Vigeland the portrayal of emotion was all-important. The struggle with form was secondary. When later on, as we shall see, he came to hold a somewhat different view of the relationship between form and feeling, his work lost in part that which had been its strength — intensity, sensitivity and tenderness. Then his grappling with form resulted in new values — greater strength, power and monumentality, but something seems to have snapped within him. Perhaps Bjørnson prophesied correctly when he said, "You cannot go on like this, Vigeland, you are burning up inside."

Zoolgical Garden 25 Juni 1951 London

Job, drawn in Paris on
New Year's Day, 1901.
Two self-portraits,
drawn in Paris on
March 17, 1901.

A RICH BUT UNHAPPY YEAR

Vigeland, who was in difficult personal circumstances, felt a desire for new experiences and a need to see the art of other lands.

In 1900 at the end of autumn he left for France and England with two stipends this time, one of which was to enable him to study Gothic art. This stipend he received from the Cathedral in Trondheim, a medieval edifice which was then under restoration. On this year-long journey we can follow him from week to week, from day to day, and even occasionally from hour to hour, owing to the hundreds of drawings he made, and which have been preserved. As a rule they are dated with great precision, showing the date, the place, and sometimes the hour. There are, however, practically no sketches of the Gothic sculpture the young man went abroad to study. No, these are drawings of the groups he dreamed of creating, of the busts he wished to model and of the monuments he hoped to erect. Above all, there are drawings for the work which was to be the heart of his oeuvre, *The Fountain*, which began to take shape in his mind at this time.

In Paris Vigeland met the playwright Gunnar Heiberg. Heiberg wrote of his visits to the young artist's miserable little hotel room, *where every day for eight days I spent some of the most interesting hours of my life ... He allowed me to sit and leaf through his drawings. Oh, how unpainter-like they were, how evident it was that they were drawn by a sculptor.*

Gunnar Heiberg was so excited by the sketches for the fountain that he wrote a flaming appeal to the good citizens of Kristiania (Oslo) urging them to seize this golden opportunity and see to it that the Fountain be erected. Then the city would no longer be called Kristiania, but simply "The City with the Fountain." His article made a tremendous impact back in Norway.

If Gunnar Heiberg found it exciting to go through Vigeland's turn-of-the-century drawings, it is even more exciting for us today. For in these drawings the seeds of practically all of Vigeland's later work are present — the majority of his statues, all of his fountain groups and a great many of his other works in bronze and stone. We are confronted by an imagination so overwhelming that we can only submit to it with admiration. Here are warmth, emotion and strength bespeaking great humanity, and here too are the pessimism and the melancholy which accompanied him throughout the greater part of his productive life. Only rarely do we meet the bitterness and brute force which can be observed in his later works, and which appear frequently in the drawings of the latter years.

Vigeland did not always take time to elaborate these early sketches. They are hasty thematic notations, jotted down at the moment the idea was born, mere memory aids for later use. Their formal qualities are not always of any particular interest, but for Vigeland they were a main-spring of ideas from which he would later draw. This is why it is such an exhilarating experience to follow his progress during this year, seeing how his ideas intertwine — how his study for a statue of Norway's

Gunnar Heiberg. March 28, 1905.

national poet Henrik Wergeland is sometimes borne up by genii as in the Abel monument, and is sometimes surrounded by figures, forming the ring which later appeared in his *Wheel of Life*. Or again, one day (August 6, 1901) we suddenly find the poet Wergeland standing under a tree. It was on this very day that the idea of the Man and the Tree — the Tree of Life — was born, and this idea eventually became the recurrent theme of *The Fountain*. It is no coincidence that the idea for Man and the Tree of Life was inspired in Vigeland by Norway's celebrated lyric poet.

However the Abel, Wergeland and Fountain motifs were not the only to intermesh. We find the poet Welhaven, Wergeland's great contemporary, being swept up and carried aloft by the people, just as Bjørnstjerne Bjørnson was to be depicted in one of Vigeland's later studies. We find the composer Edvard Grieg sitting naked on a rocky mountain-side, playing an invisible piano, similar to the study Vigeland later did of another composer, Nordraak, but which was unfortunately never executed. Vigeland even toyed with the idea of a National Monument in this bounteous year. Above a group consisting of 114 figures (Vigeland's own note) a monolith was to arise, crowned by a symbolical figure holding the Norwegian Constitution. When later asked where the idea of the Monolith came from, Vigeland answered that it had several sources. He spoke of the deep impression the art of India had made on him, he mentioned that as a child he had often carved knives with figures twisting in spirals up the handle, and he also mentioned the incident of the rolled-up photograph of *The Resurrection*.

At any rate the idea of the Monolith was already germinal in these turn-of-the-century sketches. Perhaps it was "in the air" as well. Nietzsche, who was admired by Vigeland's entire circle, had recorded his visions in one of the most poetical books written by any philosopher since Plato. In "Thus Spoke Zarathustra" he had shown tormented humanity struggling upwards towards the light, trampling on others and in turn

Drawing for a
national
monument.
Paris,
Nov. 19, 1900.
Wergeland in a
tree. Wells,
August 6, 1901.

being trampled on. "Generation trampled on generation," he
wrote. Nietzsche may have been a source of inspiration to
Vigeland or he may have served as a confirmation of the
thoughts which already occupied the sculptor and which
occupied Edvard Munch as well. This was the period when
Munch was working on his *Mountain of Men.*

Moreover, there is also a series of sketches conceived in these
Paris days which shows that Vigeland was already thinking
of the series of groups he would later do, and to which he gave
the collective title *Man and Woman* (p. 41).

Are we to conclude that Vigeland was not interested in the
works of art he saw or in the Gothic art he was supposed to
study? It is as hasty as it is wrong to decide that simply because
his drawings reveal nothing, he was interested only in his
own art. His notebooks tell another story. They abound in
observations made in museums and at exhibitions, in cathedrals
and before statues in parks. They are extremely personal
and apt.

49

There is another source of information too which tells how intensely absorbed he was by all the art he saw. This source was the letters, no fewer than 148 in number, which Vigeland wrote to his friend and patron Sophus Larpent, a Dane who was living in Oslo. The two were such close friends at the time that it was to Larpent Vigeland entrusted the arrangements for his divorce, after a brief marriage. It is not surprising then that these letters bear the stamp of being written during a time of great unhappiness. And yet, when he wrote of the impression the Gothic cathedrals made on him he was sometimes carried to heights where words take flight, where vision gains perspective and where he could forget his own worries and all the rancour he felt towards his fellow beings:

And now to the Chartres church. The central porch ... is surrounded by the apostles, and between the doors, in front of the pillar dividing the door in two, stands Christ. These apostles are quite different in character from those of Notre Dame. The latter seem like rich men, well-bred, smooth and distinguished. I might almost say they were Thorvaldsen-like if their drapery were not so scant. If each of the Notre Dame apostles had ten metres more cloth to their robes they would resemble Thorvaldsen's, and if they had still another ten metres of robe they would look like Michelsen's (a Norwegian sculptor).

The apostles of Chartres are another breed. They are more like the apostles as I imagine them, dirty and louse-infested. There is no telling what they will do in the next minute, and it is not at all sure that they will behave properly. You stand underneath them and wait, yes listen — in case something should happen.

Arriving in London, Vigeland was overwhelmed by the Parthenon sculptures. *I ought to write something about the Parthenon sculptures, but I cannot seem to manage it while I am here. I can only say that it is the greatest art there is, that it thrills me more than all the art of the whole world, including the things (I have seen) in Naples.*

Landscape from Vigeland's window. Chartres.

Thus it is that while I am there rejoicing over the figures in the tympanum, the metopes and the frieze, I suddenly get such an urge I cannot control it. There I am with my hands longing to get started on something — and they cannot. Not at all because I am here, far away, without a studio. No, it is mainly because I have no expectations of getting work soon, because I see nothing on the horizon which I can look forward to. Everything is so vague.

It makes me feel so hopeless and far away, removes me still further from my studio which is everything to me.

It is sunny here, the weather good. But what does the sun mean to me just now?

A mere button — a shiny one — stuck up in the attic.

Yours sincerely
Gustav Vigeland

He returned repeatedly to the British Museum and then wrote:

I keep thinking about Phidias' things.

Phidias was absolutely unique in Greece. Polycletus, Lysippus, Scopas and Praxiteles notwithstanding. Even Polycletus has something anxious both in form and idea, something sterile. And the others, who were supposed to have produced more "living" works, how tame they are. Even Scopas with his pathos is weak and miserly in the expansion of his figures. No, for me, of all the Greeks there is only Phidias. And the only one after him who dared to break all the bonds of human movements was Michelangelo. Not even Signorelli did it. Donatello had something quite different — the sharply cut form of the smaller details, whereas the large-scale design of his figures as a whole always had, or h a s rather, something impoverished about it.

In recent times art is supposed to have made such great progress. Phidias and Michelangelo are considered to be passé etc. And what have the so-called "daring" innovators gained? Almost nothing. They all stick to the "late Greek" positions, nothing more. They lay the figure down, but what of it? Phidias did that also, and he did it as no one has been able to do since him — not even Michelangelo. For even Michelangelo himself becomes dry, woody and gaunt beside Phidias. It is as though Michelangelo had made up a system. He did not, as Phidias did, let the form move freely, ignoring rules, ever new, with new life and new form.

And yet I am more drawn to Michelangelo. But not exactly for his form. It is his attitude, his heavy spirit, which attracts me.

I stand there looking at Phidias' things — but I am not capable of seeing in t h a t way. The sunny joy, the youthful pleasure in living forms and in life which belong to Phidias and no one else, these I cannot completely grasp. For me there are so many other things here on this earth.

Woman with skull. Drawn in Reims on May 15, 1901.

Here for the first time I was able to really see the groups from the tympanum of the Poseidon side. There is one figure, only a torso, which I place above all the others, Hermes. If one is going to speak of daringness in a work's entirety, in largescale design, then there is no other figure on earth which is superior to this one. And the smaller aspects of its form are also without an equal. How I would like to have seen the whole figure fresh upon completion.

Of the later Greek figures all, yes all of them, have a ballet-dancing air about them . . .

That Hermes torso confirmed me in what was already a very strong conviction: that no bounds should be set for what

53

*may or may not be done. As long as it really is art. The slightest
bit which is taken away, whether from the whole or a part, is a
sin. That is what the Hermes torso tells us . . .*

But he has small appreciation for the English art at the
Royal Academy:

*But what is all this? Left-overs. The kneeling knight, the
child saying good-night or praying, "touching" little dogs,
angels round the cradle, angels round the table, sentimental
titles and such-like, all of it. I saw the pictures in London, and
they were terrible, every one of them. They filled many large
rooms.* He also reacted against what was then modern French
art: *In France you will not see the good little boy with light
shining on his hair, his buttons, his shoes. There, as I said, you
will see women. And only women. Oh, those stomachs and hips
from Paris. Always they are painted most and best. There the
artist loitered longest. He hurried over the other places to get
to that which is interesting, spicy. And it is so obvious that he
works best, and truest to himself, on the abdomen and there-
abouts.*

*Naturally I would rather see a French exhibition than an
English one. Instead of all that nauseous Sunday-school morality
I would rather have all these inflated female bottoms in front
of me. It is at least something, even if one does soon get tired
of them. At any rate they show a little technique, dexterity,
a stylish arrangement which is momentarily striking. Although
by the time you are home, you have forgotten everything,
except that you were cheated . . . It all fades into prettiness,
delicacy, sophistication. And in this silken web they scurry
about and spin exquisitely.*

*It is quite certain that I have learned something from Gothic
art which classical art could not have taught me. All things
taken together I have profited more from this journey than
from any other I have ever undertaken. So when everything
clarifies a little and I get it all into perspective, why then
things will be better.*

The irate Ibsen.

PORTRAITS

Gustav Vigeland created a veritable Norwegian Pantheon with all the busts he made of famous contemporaries. We find here almost everybody of any importance in the intellectual life of Vigeland's own and the preceding generation. There can be no doubt that Vigeland deliberately intended to fashion an image of the age which would live on in the awareness of future generations. Among his drawings and papers several long lists have been found enumerating the eminent men he had already made busts of, together with other lists showing the busts he hoped to make. His models were sometimes personal friends, for in his youth Vigeland was often in the company of artists and writers. Only later did he withdraw into his legendary isolation. The majority of the busts which he made in the nineties were not commissions. Rather, Vigeland made them because their subjects fascinated him. These busts in particular, with their penetrating characterization and their bold treatment of form, engrave themselves on the memory.

Few Norwegian sculptors have been able to read faces as the young Vigeland could. That which we only suspect to lie behind the features, which we perhaps catch only a glimpse of — it is just that which he brings out, holds fast and emphasizes. In his best busts he states something unfailingly true about each of the individuals he portrays. However this truth is not that which a mask taken from life would tell. On the contrary, it has been fashioned by a strong artistic will which intuitively grasped the essence of the sitter — that which creates character. Anyone with a perceptive mind can see in Vigeland's portraits not only what the models looked like, but how they actually were. Many of those he modelled were surely foreign to his nature and not always congenial to work with, and yet something in their faces captivated him. He had to get past the outer shell and into the core.

Two examples of the greatly differing busts he produced in the nineties are those of *Oscar Nissen,* a physician and philanthropist, and the poet *Sigbjørn Obstfelder.* Oscar Nissen's bust is loaded with energy. The raised head grows organically out of the shoulders. His definite features are modelled solidly and convincingly, particularly the jutting, strong-willed jaw and the decidedly closed mouth. Yet, most impressive of all are the observant eyes smouldering in the deep shadows of the hawk-like brows. Here Vigeland depicts not only the idealist, but also the active politician who fought for those ideals, the admonisher and prosecutor who attacked injustice. The bust has been given its rightful place in Folkets Hus, the trade union headquarters. It bears the date, Christmas Eve, 1896 (p. 58).

During that year Vigeland had also modelled Obstfelder. Here the refined profile is only partly freed from the dark

Sigbjørn Obstfelder, 1895. Oscar Nissen, Dec. 24, 1896.

mass of the clay. This jaw also juts forwards, but it is not energetic or vigorous. The sensitive head on the long slender neck conveys an impression of awareness, and this is intensified by the luxurious moustache. An air of listening is conveyed by the delicately formed shell of the ear.

Such works typify the scope of young Vigeland's portrait art, where the bold energy of perception is paired with the delicate sensitivity of compassion.

Both sitters were his close personal friends. Oscar Nissen and his wife Fernanda were influential in working for Vigeland's recognition. As early as 1899 Oscar Nissen had written: *Gustav Vigeland's art cries out for better conditions for Norwegian sculpture. We are confronted here by a rich talent which ought to be assisted, given a chance to flourish, the opportunity to work independently as the artist's powers*

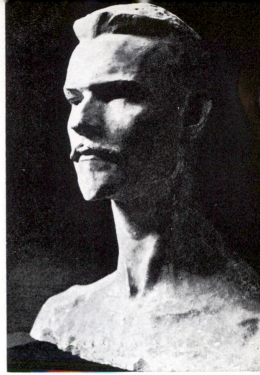

Harald Sohlberg. Signed Nov. 17, 1892. Jens Thiis, 1893—94.

dictate. Nissen describes *Hell*, the principal work of Vigeland's youth thus: *It seems to draw to itself the essence of all that is implacable in life. In the midst of his kingdom Satan sits enthroned ... Human suffering has found sublime expression here, imbued with the beauty which flows from profound emotion. As the procession passes by hands are raised with shrieks of supplication for grace from the relentless, cold, stony Satan who sits aloft, his elbows on his knees and his hard chin resting on his tightly clenched fist. The implacable one* (p. 27).

Obviously the critic who wrote thus must have been in very close contact with the artist. Just how close is revealed by the fact that Vigeland asked his friend Oscar Nissen to let him borrow his distinctive features for Satan. Permission was evidently granted, for there is a visible resemblance between Satan and the great humanitarian Oscar Nissen. In fact, Vigeland's Satan is not the prince of evil but the brooding one, the sufferer and co-sufferer.

The busts of two other early friends, the painter *Harald Sohlberg* and *Jens Thiis,* the art historian, date from the years 1892 to 1894. They were created in a neo-romantic spirit, and both have a vague dreaming, "veiled" air about them as Vigeland himself said. He hollowed out the eyes and then bored even deeper for the pupils — a technique which he otherwise seldom used. The art nouveau preference for long slender lines finds expression in his emphasis on the subjects' long necks.

In 1896, when he was 27 years old, he modelled his brother *Emanuel,* six years his junior. The likeness must have been considerable. Comparing it with a Danish bust showing Gustav Vigeland at about the same age, we find a striking family resemblance. In this work Vigeland was clearly influenced by Florentine art of the Renaissance. When looking at the bust of Emanuel with his broad, bare shoulders, one is immediately made to think of Donatello's *Gattamelata's Son.* At that time the brothers were friends; later in life they no longer saw one another. Here, however, the elder brother did a sensitive and affectionate portrait of the younger. It contains an unusual combination of youthful openness and thoughtful introspection which makes it especially expressive. The sharply cutoff shoulder area was borrowed, as noted, from Renaissance busts. At first glance the work appears unified and solidly constructed, but when the treatment of the sinews and muscles of the neck are compared with Donatello's, it must be admitted that Vigeland's formal statement of the neck and shoulder parts is not convincing enough.

Writing in 1907 on the subject of Vigeland's portraits, the Danish connoisseur of art Francis Beckett had this to say: *Not since the days of the Renaissance has the treatment of the surface been so incomparably lively. The best of (these works) need not fear being placed alongside the Donatello busts which Vigeland was acquainted with . . . Now that Meunier is*

Vigeland's brother, Emanuel. Sept. 10, 1896.

dead and Rodin is so old and mannered, Vigeland stands forth as undisputedly the greatest sculptor Europe possesses.

When he was in Paris in 1901 Vigeland modelled the two authors who were to be constantly in the forefront as champions for his cause — the one exerting the influence of a national father-figure, the other using his brilliant pen. They were *Bjørnstjerne Bjørnson* and *Gunnar Heiberg* (p. 47).

At the beginning, Vigeland, who was then a shy and lonely 32-year old, was not particularly elated by the commission to do a Bjørnson bust, and he dreaded going to meet the man. The day after he began working on it however, he wrote enthusiastically to his friend Larpent, "He is magnificent!"

Drawing for an Ibsen mausoleum, to be erected on a rocky isle in the Oslo fiord P. 63: Bjørnstjerne Bjørnson, 1901.

The Bjørnson bust is the most monumental bust Vigeland ever made. It sets before us the open, active, extroverted popular leader that he was. With its simplified form the bust is intended for marble and not, as in previous busts, for bronze. It is like several of Vigeland's busts from the nineties in including the shoulder portions. Vigeland obviously aimed for, and achieved, an aura of classical heroicness found in none of his earlier portraits. The powerful personality of the almost 70-year old Bjørnson made a strong impression on the young sculptor.

The Heiberg bust, made the same year, is of a wholly different character. Strangely enough Vigeland included the tie, whereas he usually omitted all such dated details (p. 47).

Heiberg has recorded his astonishment on first meeting Vigeland when, one spring day in 1901, a young man knocked at his door in Paris and said, "I have come straight from Bjørnson where they were all calling you names. Will you

let me become acquainted with you? My name is Gustav Vigeland." After this highly unconventional introduction a warm friendship was established between the two, which on Heiberg's side lasted until his death. As late as 1924, not long before he died, he defended Vigeland against the attacks which were then seriously beginning. Heiberg concluded the article he then wrote in Vigeland's defense thus, "He is the one and only 'One and Only' we have."

In another article Heiberg once told what it was like to pose for Vigeland. *He started modelling me. He cast his eyes on my face and then back to the wet clay. He nailed me down with his eyes, and if I did not collapse each time he looked away, it was because I feared the next moment when I would have that terrible gaze full in the face again. I neither dozed nor itched all over my body as I had done whenever I posed before. I felt as though I were a poor corpse and he a crook-backed hyena with eyes which never stood still, devouring everything, yet always famish-hed. The fact that the bust en-ded up resembling a cruel Ro-man emperor must have come partly from my unheroic bear-ing. I might add that he rejected it.*

It is true that the first version does bear a faint resemblance to a Caracalla bust, and it is also true that Vigeland disowned it and did a new one in 1905.

When Vigeland returned from his year-long journey in 1901 he made his first bust of *Henrik Ibsen.* How different is the portrait of this wrathful old dramatist, reserved and fierce, from that of the open, extro-verted Bjørnson. Ibsen was be-ing sculpted against his will, and he did not at all like having his immaculate sitting-room dir-tied by Vigeland's trestles, tubs and wet clay. "I must go to the barber first!" he protested. "No," the sculptor replied, "we'll take the solid parts first." This rejoinder struck the aging poet so forcibly that he re-mained seated, mumbling to himself, "The solid parts first, hmm — the solid parts first." However, Vigeland was not per-mitted to complete the bust in

P. 64: Edvard Grieg being mo-delled. January 1903.
This page: Ibsen in flaming garments. Drawing for a mo-nument. April 30, 1902.

front of his model. In 1903 he made a new bust which is now in Oslo's National Theatre. It is made of marble, a material which is not really suited to the detailed, impressionistic style of the bust (p. 57).

One suspects that its was precisely Ibsen's wrath that goaded Vigeland into portraying him as the inexorable indicter of society who turns his searching gaze on mankind with sullen ire. The large right eye is electrifying, while the smaller left eye is pinched together in a squint, and the set of the mouth shows embittered strength. The hair is blown over the forehead like threatening clouds over a steep mountain. The firmly shaped skull can be sensed beneath the great mane of hair which, together with Ibsen's characteristic beard, inevitably suggests an old lion.

The following year Vigeland fashioned the bust which he personally ranked higher than all the others — that of Norway's great linguistic scholar *Sophus Bugge*. "If I may say so myself, this bust is without spot or blemish. It was this bust which opened the way for me." There is an air of calm reflection about this pouchy yet firmly modelled face where life has ploughed deep furrows. The eyes seem distant. They are not directed outwards but sink inwards in the world of contemplation existing behind the high and noble brow. Although the hair flickers restlessly upwards, it only emphasizes the calm of the thoughtful features.

The impressionistic bust of the critic *Carl Nærup* is alive and spontaneous. Vigeland has captured the model's delighted pleasure at one of his own elegant witticisms. One almost hears his faintly snuffling, chanting voice and his peculiar clucking laughter which, once heard, was never forgotten.

As a portrayer of character it may be that Vigeland probed most deeply in the bust of the aged novelist *Jonas Lie* — a work which he fashioned with brilliant assurance. The skin is taut and thin upon the cranium. The skull-cap which Lie habitually wore is eliminated. Vigeland had little fondness for such

66

Sophus Bugge. April 14, 1902. Carl Nærup. April 11, 1904.

external attributes. There is something searching, almost visionary in the nearsighted gaze, and the trembling mouth of this
old man is expressive of great feeling (p. 69).

Vigeland's later portraits never again attained the same
psychological depth. He gradually moved away from his early
painter-like style which could be so expressive, and strove
consciously for a more balanced, a quieter form. Yet strangely
enough, when contemplating the busts of the early years one
has a strong sense of their cohesion and integrity, in spite of
their impressionistic, sketchy style. This is not nearly so evident
in the later works where Vigeland adopted a more austere
style, and where he took as his formal ideals the portrait busts
of ancient Rome. Certain of these later works were actually
done in the classical herma form (p. 156).

Drawing for a bust of Jonas Lie.
P. 69: Jonas Lie. July 27, 1904.

The *self-portrait* of 1922 shows us Vigeland at the time when he signed the contract with the city of Oslo. Here he is purposeful, self-assured, fully aware of his own worth and still in his prime. Nevertheless, there is something about his self-confident expression which betrays an inner insecurity. Reserved and severe, he repulses all who might try to penetrate his exterior. What was otherwise his strong point as a portraitist — showing what lay behind the facade — was just what he refused to do here. There is something curiously mask-like about these rigorously stern features (p. 155).

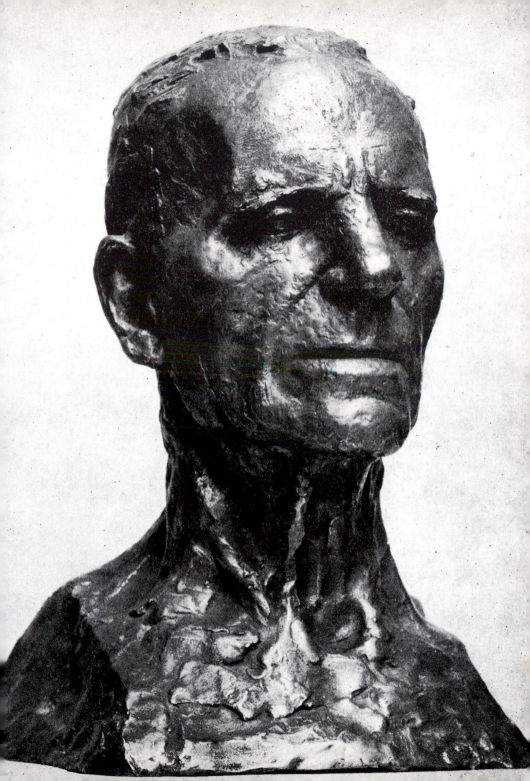

P. 70: Monument to Niels Henrik Abel.
Erected in Oslo in 1908.
This page: Inside the artist's old studio
at Hammersborg.

THE COMMEMORATIVE STATUES

The beginning of the century was a period abounding in competitions and commissions for large commemorative works. Vigeland was prepared for the challenge, as he had been working out ideas for statues of various famous Norwegians for quite some time.

The tiny studio which he then had was by no means suited to such large tasks. Abel, the subject of the group Vigeland was working on, could not pick up any speed on his flight underneath the plaster rosettes of the studio's ceiling, so Vigeland set about looking for a proper studio. He found a ramshackle little house which the city turned over him.

Here however, the rain poured in, fungi as large as fists grew on the walls, and though Vigeland kept the stove red hot the clay froze, forcing him to spend several hours a day

71

Vigeland in his studio on Sept. 9, 1903, and taking a rest — July 27, 1903.

thawing it out before he could begin to work. In this place Vigeland lived and worked from 1902 until 1923, when he moved into the building that is now his museum. In 1908 the city had an addition built on to the old studio, making conditions there considerably better. Nevertheless, it gradually grew more and more crowded with studies waiting to be executed on a larger scale. The idyllic little garden overflowed with bronze tree-groups. In addition to all this the large granite groups began to take shape (p. 136—137).

It was in this tumble-down shack that Vigeland fashioned those works which will doubtless remain as landmarks of Norwegian sculpture, and which assured him an unshakable position in the esteem of his fellow-countrymen. It was here that he created *Abel, Beethoven, Wergeland,* Wergeland's sister the feminist pioneer *Camilla Collett* and *Nordraak,* the com-

Two studies for the Abel monument, 1902.

poser of the Norwegian national anthem. It was also this period
which saw the birth of nearly all his most important busts.

ABEL

The first "Vigeland affair" was the discussion surrounding
the monument to *Niels Henrik Abel*. It began in 1902 when
the committee of judges passed on the 19 models submitted,
and lasted until Vigeland's group was erected near the driveway
leading to the Royal Palace, in 1908. Even after the unveiling,
the battle continued to rage.

The controversy it aroused is understandable. Abel bears no
resemblance to what Vigeland so contemptuously called a
"frock-coat man." The sculptor's portrayal of the great mathematician who died so young is by no means naturalistic. Instead
he made an apotheosis to science itself, to genius. The 32-year

old Vigeland may well have had himself in mind as much as Abel when he created this daringly devised young genius soaring through space and time, borne by the genii of thought and spirit. Vigeland had a high opinion of his own capacities. He considered himself an exceptional person, and if he had not done so he would hardly have managed to create all that he did.

It was the University of Oslo which sponsored the competition for the Abel memorial, and a portrait statue was requested. It was originally intended to stand near the steps ,of the University. Vigeland strove loyally to conform to the specifications. He tried to make a portrait statue but, like his competitors, he had only an old drawing to work from. He felt more and more dishonest in his attempts to make a portrait without knowing what the person had looked like. It is

74

P. 74: Sketch of Abel's head, Dec. 18, 1901, and the drawing by Johan
Gørbitz on which Abel's likeness was to be based.
This page: Abel's head as done by Vigeland.

Michelangelo: Allegory of Victory.

absorbing to follow Vigeland's progress through the more than 150 sketches where he carries on a discussion with himself, trying to find a solution.

Back in the eighteen-nineties Vigeland had already toyed with the idea of making an Abel statue. He visualized first a man erect, wearing a long coat, then a man striding along in the same coat (December 1900). Here already, he had arrived at one of the central aspects of the finished work, for he wrote on the sketch, "shooting forwards, as though he were cleaving the air . . ." Half a year later there is a winged spirit flying behind Abel, who is now nude. By the following year (December 1901), the idea of Abel being borne aloft was clear in his mind, though as yet there was only one genie, now wingless.

When the competition was announced in 1902 Vigeland began to make studies in the round, and it can be seen how he tried to keep within the stipulations which had been made. Abel had died in 1829, and Vigeland showed him seated, wearing clothes of that period, and compared to the final version this is a very conventional study indeed. That very same day however (August 5, 1902), Vigeland did another study of him disrobed. Next we see how some drapery

Abel in progress, Sept. 19, 1903.

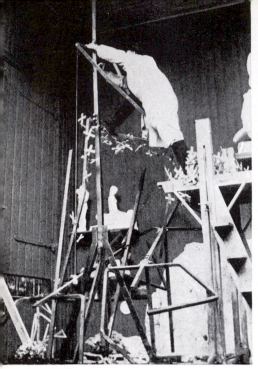

1. The iron framework being erected on April 20, 1903.

2. Two days later.

3. May 1, 1903.

4. May 14—Sept. 19, 1903. Note the Welhaven statue (now lost) in lower right-hand corner.

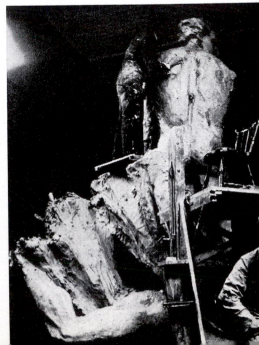

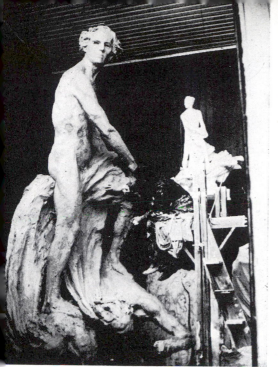

5. Sept. 19, 1903.

6. Sept. 2, 1904. Abel wrapped in wet cloths.

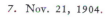

7. Nov. 21, 1904.

8. Feb. 25, 1905.

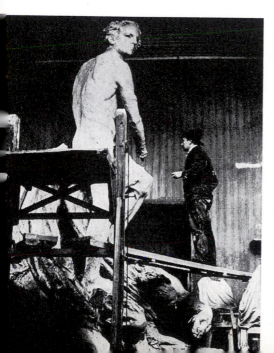

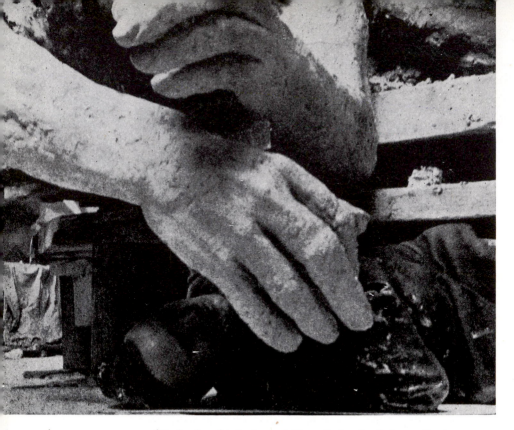

Vigeland on his back, modelling the hands of the genii.

is made to billow out behind him, creating movement. Then
he is shown erect, the drapery forming a background.

His model won no prize. First prize went to the very compe-
tent sculptor Ingebrigt Vik, who had the misfortune to be a
contemporary of Vigeland. Though Vigeland received neither
second nor third prize there were, however, people on the
jury with an artistic conscience. Two of them, prominent
Norwegian painters, supported Vigeland's entry on the grounds
that it was "artistically superior to the others." But the final
decision of the jury as a whole was that "they could not
recommend that any of the entries be erected."

A number of Norway's leading intellectuals came forth on
behalf of Vigeland and in 1903 Vigeland began modelling the

monument full-scale at his own expense. For twenty-five long months he did battle with the fifteen-foot high colossus. He spent the summer high up on the scaffolding shaping Abel's tremendous body with his small tools. As Michelangelo worked lying on his back beneath the ceiling of the Sistine Chapel, so Vigeland lay on the floor of his studio under the massive arms of the genii.

In speaking of Michelangelo it might be mentioned that all who are acquainted with his *Victory* will find that the Abel group is reminiscent of it. Vigeland was aware of the resemblance, and once said to a friend of his: *It is unintentional. I was not thinking about the "Victory" when I was modelling Abel. It was only later that the resemblance struck me* (p. 76).

In December 1904 the committee made known that Vigeland's model would be purchased, and in the autumn of 1908 the monument was unveiled on the promontory near the approach to the Royal Palace. There, on what is now called Abel Hill, it has stood proudly for more than half a century. And up to this very day it remains Oslo's most imaginative monument.

Two 'Abel' drawings.

30 mai 1897

WERGELAND

The two wingless figures which carry Abel on his flight were termed "genii" by Vigeland. This vague concept, these genii, occur constantly in the artist's works — only occasionally in the finished works, more frequently in the studies in the round and repeatedly in the drawings. As a rule these genii are symbols of poetic inspiration, sometimes of germination and growth, and occasionally they simply symbolize ideas themselves. The first time the genii appear in a dated sketch is in the 1897 drawing for a Wergeland statue. The poet is wearing a cloak and stands on a broad pedestal. This conception does not differ too much from the Wergeland statue done by Bergslien, Vigeland's early teacher. Here, however, there are several vague figures draped in long robes behind the main figure. In the succeeding years Vigeland made a great many drawings, dated and undated, for a Wergeland statue, and in these the genie-figures are further elaborated. Frequently the ideas for the Abel group encroach upon the Wergeland theme with the result that Wergeland can also be seen to be carried by one or more genii. There is often a whole circle of genii around

83

Two drawings for a Wergeland monument. Study for a Wergeland monument. May 9, 1922. P. 85: The head of the Wergeland statue.

him. This motif was revived in the 1920's and finally became *The Wheel of Life,* one of Vigeland's last works (p. 149).

Among the turn-of-the-century drawings entitled Wergeland there are some where the work is given the shape of a bowl, somewhat like the later *Giant Bowl* of the Fountain. Moreover, there is an interesting drawing dated August 6, 1901 where Wergeland and another figure indicated as Welhaven stand naked under a tree. This drawing is obviously related to the Fountain tree-group which Vigeland called *The Dreamer,* a man who stands dreaming under a canopy of branches. It is fascinating to watch such ideas being born and see them interacting, and to observe how much of Vigeland's later production was already latent in the drawings of the late nineties and the countless sketches from the 1900—1901 year of travel. One of the main groups of drawings, and one where ideas proliferate in abundance, is precisely that composed

The head of the Wergeland statue and Wergeland's death mask.

of drawings depicting Wergeland. Long before any monument to that poet had been proposed, Vigeland was dreaming of creating a memorial to Norway's great lyric poet whom he loved so well (p. 49).

It is not possible to follow here all the stages of development the Wergeland theme underwent on the way to the finished statue. We can only note that a long series of sketches and studies leads to the final composition, and that Vigeland made constant use of genii here to symbolize poetic inspiration. Many statements made by Vigeland at later dates suggest that in his own case as well, he felt there were powers outside him which inspired his ideas. "I was driven and lashed onwards by powerful forces outside myself."

As we have seen above, Vigeland must surely have been thinking of himself as well when he fashioned the Abel monument's celebration of genius. Similarly, he must have felt a kinship with the other distinguished intellectuals and artists he directed his attention to — the great lone figures who cleared the path for others to follow. However, from the day when the Wergeland memorial committee addressed itself to Vigeland, his ideas could no longer live their own independent life in his imagination. They acquired a more concrete form, and it was obvious that the artist felt himself restrained by the commission to do a historical personage. He dropped the symbols and no longer had Wergeland being carried through space. On the contrary, he had the poet stand and clothed him in the severe knee-length coat and narrow trousers of the period. Thus he made what he had so scornfully called a "frock-coat man." Yet, amazingly, Vigeland actually managed to combine a supremely realistic image of the man Wergeland with a symbolic representation of the poet at the very moment of inspired lyric conception. And all this was done without any theatrical effects. He merely turned Wergeland's face upwards and closed his eyes, with the result that the poet seems to be attuned to the infinite with all his senses. For one brief moment Vigeland captured the poet's soul, and we realize that as Wergeland said, "There is a kinship between the soul and the stars."

It is hard to believe that this head with all its aliveness and its intelligence was made from a death mask! Nevertheless there are many small details which indicate that Vigeland took the poet's death mask as a starting point. There is the hair which clings damply to the forehead, and is not parted on the side one sees in Wergeland's portraits, but on the same side as in the death mask. Then there is the ruffled eyebrow and the slightly humped nose, not to mention the angle of the head, which is exactly the same as that of the mask when placed horizontally on a table. The artist softened the traces of death which are so evident in the mask, and at the same time he re-created Nature's own work with fidelity and sensitivity. The result is the most inspired head in all of Norwegian sculpture.

The statue was unveiled in both Kristiansand and Fargo, North Dakota, on June 17, 1908, the hundredth anniversary of Wergeland's birth. Few Norwegian works of art have been such an inspiration to later generations of artists as has Vigeland's *Wergeland*.

Drawings, dated Oct. 17, 1902 and Dec. 21, 1902, for a commemorative statue of Camilla Collett.

CAMILLA COLLETT

The women I like best are those who are so constantly engrossed in their household duties that only the tips of their noses show, Vigeland once said. Upon the same occasion, imbued as he was with the spirit of the nineties, he expressed his abomination of 'la belle Hélène,' saying that it was *ghastly what a woman could drive a man to do.* As for blue-stockings, he detested them.

It is all the more remarkable then that one of his loveliest commemorative statues is of a woman, and a militant woman at that.

In the Palace Park in Oslo, under lofty branches, stands *Camilla Collett.* It is perhaps best to see her on a cold autumn day when the trees are bare and whipped by the wind, for there is an autumnal quality about this statue which reflects Camilla Collett's lone struggle in bitter isolation and adversity.

"In the Storm," Vigeland called it. In this brilliant formulation he has the storm clutch at her skirts, the great, soft billowing lines creating an expressive, sweeping rhythm which is almost Gothic in feeling. Alone, old and shivering, she draws

Drawing for the Camilla Collett commemorative statue, dated Dec. 21, 1902. Study for the Camilla Collett statue, May 8, 1906.

her fringed shawl round her narrow shoulders and bends before the gusts of the storm. The same bowing motion is repeated in the willow branches of the low wrought iron fence enclosing the statue. "Poor lady, tired and cold and ill," said the author's five-year-old daughter when walking one day in the Palace Park. The child had grasped the artist's intention — to express loneliness and the cold through simple and direct means.

It had taken a long time however, before Vigeland arrived at this straightforward solution. The evolution of this masterpiece can be traced through more than 120 sketches. We can watch the various ideas as they are conceived and then rejected or developed in his mind. In his original conception Camilla Collett was to be seated on a high, wave-like base, and several drawings bear the inscription, "The figures on the base will be women awakening," or again, "The awakening of the women." Other pages show him considering the idea of a double statue of Camilla Collett and her contemporary, the poet Welhaven, with whom she had been intimate for a period. This idea was soon abandoned in favour of the young Camilla as she was painted by her father Nicolai Wergeland. She was to be dressed in crinolines and wear a summery straw hat

Detail of the statue, and a photograph of Camilla Collett in 1886.

tied beneath her chin. In this medium-sized study in the round she is holding a tear-drenched handkerchief in her right hand, her left being pressed to her heart. It did not take long, however, before this sentimental portrayal was superceded by the militant feminist. Raising a closed umbrella, she stands ready to strike. This drawing resembles Vigeland's lively little study of another feminist, *Aasta Hansteen*. Later, the old and indignant polemicist is replaced by the young widow Camilla Collett, the author of the first major Norwegian novel written by a woman, "Amtmannens Døtre" (The Governor's Daughters).

Vigeland finally decided to show us Camilla Collett as an old woman. Here she is not the militant pioneer who wrote "From the Camp of the Silent Ones." Quite the opposite, the sculptor has emphasized all that was frail in her being. This lonely woman has fought the fight to the end and is looking back upon a long and difficult life.

On the statue's pedestal can be seen the inscription "Erected by Women." In fact, the decision to hold a competition in 1902 and invite Norwegian artists to enter it was the result of a fund-raising petition signed by 500 influential Norwegian women.

The Camilla Collett memorial. 1909.
Erected in bronze in the Palace Park, Oslo, in 1911.

The final choice lay between Vik and Vigeland, with the majority supporting the latter. It vas the second time the talented and sensitive sculptor was outshone by Vigeland, who was two years his junior.

27 Sut 1902

NORDRAAK AND BEETHOVEN

In 1902, the year the *Abel* group was created, Vigeland was commissioned to make a commemorative statue of *Rikard Nordraak,* the composer of Norway's national anthem. To this end Edvard Grieg had collected 5,000 crowns by giving various benefit concerts. It was first intended that Vigeland do a bust. He made one, of colossal dimensions, but did not like it and destroyed it. Then he decided upon a symbolical representation of Nordraak, and he made several studies of a large, naked figure seated on a rocky mountain-side, posed as though he were playing a piano. An old photograph shows that this version was enlarged to gigantic proportions. Grieg, however, did not approve. He found it far too daring and unconventional, and wanted a likeness of Nordraak instead. Thereupon Vigeland modelled a standing portrait statue. The sculptor has

P. 92: The Pianist, intended to commemorate Rikard Nordraak, but never erected. Clay figure in giant format. Drawing dated Oct. 27, 1902. This page: Rikard Nordraak, 1905. Unveiled in Oslo on Norway's national holiday, May 17, 1911. Soapstone.

related how the severe cold in his studio cracked it, so that when it was later warmed up the statue collapsed, and Vigeland had to build it up all over again.

Not only Grieg, but also Bjørnson, Nordraak's cousin, was on the committee which was to pass judgment on the statue. When the clay figure was completed, the two gentlemen came to the miserable shack Vigeland worked in to give their opinions. The first to arrive was Grieg. "No, Vigeland, you have made him far too big. Nordraak was little, like I am," said Grieg. "Oh, yes?" said Vigeland, perplexed. A few minutes later Bjørnson blustered in. "No, no, Gustav, you have made him much too little. Rikard was big, like me!"

The figure is cut in steatite (soapstone). It is one of the most naturalistic works he ever made, honestly and carefully worked, but without the soaring imagination which infuses the *Abel* group, and which the "Pianist" version would undoubtedly have had. At its present location in Wergelandsveien in Oslo, with tall buildings in the background, this statue of Norway's distinguished tone-poet may indeed seem

94

P. 94: Drawing for wrought iron railing.
This page:
Wrought iron monster in front of Nordraak memorial.

somewhat small. The stance is a conventional one, as though Nordraak were posing for a photographer, and at first glance the statue does not seem too impressive. Yet, on closer inspection one soon realizes just how firm and definite the form is.

There are weird mythical beasts of wrought iron guarding the statues, and here the artist gave his imagination free rein. It is as though these chained monsters express some of the magic which was denied expression when Vigeland had to renounce the "Pianist." In the low wrought iron fence enclosing the statue there are dragons devouring one another in a self-destroying struggle. These works strongly reflect the art nouveau style, and they demonstrate an interest in wrought iron which was later to emerge in the large, richly conceived figured gates surrounding the Monolith (p. 151).

On several of the "Pianist" sketches Vigeland wrote the name of Grieg, but he also evolved a series of other ideas for a Grieg statue. Nothing ever came of them, however. An old photograph shows that his charming little study of Grieg with his collar turned up to protect him from the cold, and

95

P. 96: Beethoven statue in progress, 1905. Erected in bronze in the courtyard of the Vigeland Museum.
This page:
Egil Skallagrimsson defying his enemies. 1922–23. In plaster in the Vigeland Museum.
Peder Claussøn Friis (1937) hurling a Catholic saint's statue into the river. Erected in bronze in Vigeland's native district, Sør Audnedal.

with his head to one side as though he were listening, was modelled large-scale. However, Vigeland destroyed it (see ill. p. 114).

In a number of other sketches Grieg is portrayed in the act of conducting, and certain of them show him surrounded by a cloud of genii. This conception was applied to the *Beethoven* statue. Here he has omitted the accessories of the Grieg sketches — both the symbolical figures and the billowing draperies — but he has retained the theme of the artist in combat. Beethoven is in the nude, his arms lifted, half fighting, half conducting His hands are closed fists making powerful groping movements. The sculptor wanted to illustrate here how art is born in rebellion and travail. In Vigeland's Beethoven the act of creation is one of ecstatic rage, bordering on dementia. One is reminded of Vigeland's words on Michelangelo: "He is bowed beneath the burden of his divine gift and creates in agony . . ."

Bjørnstjerne Bjørnson, bronze, in Bergen, 1917. Christian Michelsen, bronze, 1936, also in Bergen. Snorre Sturlason, bronze, 1938. In Bergen and Reykholt, Iceland.

OTHER STATUES

Vigeland was often drawn by the dramatic aspect of a subject. It was surely the brief but dramatic text from the Norse sagas which attracted him when he set about making a statue of the viking and skald *Egil Skallagrimsson's* gesture of defiance.

The saga relates how Egil took a pole of hazel-wood and rammed it into a crack in the rock. He set a sneering horse-head on it facing the Norwegian mainland, and before leaving in exile he called down a curse on Norway and his enemies. Vigeland took great pains to have all the historical details correct. He got Norway's noted expert on runic inscriptions, Magnus Olsen, to come to his studio and cut the runes of the anathema into the pole behind Egil. He borrowed a sword from the University's collection of antiqui-

The Clan, plaster, 1934 – 36. The Vigeland Museum 1899.

ties, and he obtained exact information on the costumes of the 900's. He made an intensive study of a slaughtered horse's head and modelled from it for some time. Eventually the head smelled so strong that it had to be buried in the garden.

Vigeland called Egil "a distorted self-portrait," and he has visibly imparted to the irate rebel some of his own features. Although he had worked on the idea earlier, the final statue was not made until 1923. At this period the criticism of his mammoth plans began to bother him because now some of his close friends and colleagues were among his critics. One of them was the city architect and another was the university's professor of art history. It was not criticism of the type which he could simply ignore. The objections, from the point of view of these two qualified members of the official committee, were certainly honest, but naturally enough the artist could not be expected to share their views. He interpreted their criticism as a betrayal by close friends. He was furious, and in his rage

99

he gave his own features to Eigil Skallagrimson as he stands there blasting curses at the Norwegian people. The two critical members of the committee which functioned as an intermediary between Vigeland and the municipality were dropped, and Vigeland continued to work on his huge project.

As in the case of Egil Skallagrimsson, Vigeland also portrayed a dramatic incident in his statue of *Peder Claussøn Friis*. Legend would have it that in his anger this powerful Reformation clergyman threw saints' statues from Catholic times into the river. It is a sorry thing indeed for this great humanist to be represented as a destroyer of works of art, and it is curious, to say the least, for a sculptor to make a memorial to an iconoclast! This statue undoubtedly possesses a certain dramatic strength, but it is nevertheless one of Vigeland's weaker works. The form lacks cohesion, and the clerical gown hangs like a sack as though there were no solid body inside it. The proportions are uncomfortably wrong, and vitality is replaced here by a kind of primitive force. The statue was erected in the 1930's as a gift from the sculptor to his native district.

Vigeland's large group *The Clan* is an elaboration of an earlier study for a proposed national monument. Later on, in the years 1934—1935 Vigeland made a full-scale version of one of these early studies with the intention of placing it in the Frogner Sculpture Park.

This populous group with its 21 figures is schematically weak, and has many of the short-comings which frequently characterize Vigeland's later works. Its colossal dimensions are more overwhelming than convincing, particularly in the case of the two identical giants who stand protectively on either side of the cluster of women, children and old people. The group is only summarily modelled, and its perfunctory treatment of form leaves much to be desired.

Horseman, gargoyle for Trondheim cathedral, north transept.

GOTHIC INTERLUDE

Ever since 1872 the restoration of the medieval cathedral in Trondheim had been under the leadership of the architect Chr. Christie. A period of 25 years was to elapse before Vigeland did his first piece of work for the church, a relief with an age-old subject, "The Adoration of the Shepherds." Although this work was never placed in the church, there were a great number of other tasks which awaited Vigeland there — so many in fact, that they seemed to be overwhelming. A note written in 1900 shows him making some bitterly arch

Rain-spout for Trondheim cathedral.
P. 103: A rain-spout and a portrait of the cathedral architect, Chr. Christie, 1899.

calculations about the amount of work expected of him, and he wonders if it will not devolve upon him to execute all of the west facade's 44 statues. *I shall be fifty years old, and by then I will be finished.*

In 1898 Vigeland began to work for the church in earnest. He was particularly intrigued by the prospect of doing 16 gargoyles for the main tower. Here he could let his imagination run riot and give vent to his visionary creativity teamed with a macabre grotesqueness similar to that of the medieval originals. There can be no doubt that Vigeland's penchant for monsters, dragons and chimeras grew out of his work with the Trondheim gargoyles. Such motifs recur frequently in his later work. However, the monsters of his early days possess a primitive vitality often lacking in the later dragon works, which tend to be more ornamental.

In a different vein altogether from the rain-spouts and gargoyles was the work connected with the ornamentation of the
chancel arch — the slender arch dating from the 15th century
which separates the nave from the choir. The airy, elegant late
Gothic architecture requires figures partaking of the same
lightness and slenderness. Vigeland submitted loyally to this
difficult task and fashioned Biblical figures of wood, some
of them polychrome, which complement the architecture in a
highly satisfactory way. Yet, they are far from being slavish
copies, and they speak the deeply personal language of the
young Vigeland. All the same, he managed to capture here
the spirit of Gothic art.

There were times however, when the views held by architect
and sculptor did not coincide. This was unavoidable. In a
letter to his friend Larpent, Vigeland wrote: *Trondheim's*

Chancel arch in Trondheim cathedral. Crucifiction group, king David and the prophet Isaiah. P. 105: The Christ of the chancel arch. This figure is situated beneath the figures shown on p. 104, 1902.

cathedral is being made too Protestant, something it has never been. Shouldn't the work there be carried out as much as possible in accordance with the spirit of those who built it?

In another letter he exclaims: *Oh, I remember so many of the details. How often haven't I wandered around with him (Christie) for hours on end looking at folds, fingers, hands, buckles, curls which he simply insisted I copy! But is it not the essence of the Gothic style which one is supposed to capture? And the aura which surrounds it?*

In the beginning Vigeland was greatly absorbed by his work on the cathedral, and he was happy to get the tasks which were assigned him. *The more I work with Gothic art the more it pleases me. I will never be wholly at home in it, nor will it change me. But I must say that it has feeling — yes, more than any other style. It may be that which allies us,* he wrote in September 1898. Late in 1900 he wrote to Professor Dietrichson from Paris, *I am looking forward to working on the Trondheim cathedral, although I will by no means stop working on my own things.* Gradually however, he lost his enthusiasm and dreaded the prospect of having to create in the style of a time which was not his own. *Here in Paris* (January 1901) *I feel more strongly than ever that I really should not get involved with the cathedral, as it will wear me out ahead of time and encroach on my own work. I once said that I would look on it as a rest. Mere words! What a rest that would be! To unhinge oneself, force one's eyes to see as the Gothics saw —*

Angel killing a dragon.
Relief for the nave.
P. 107: Vigeland's 'studio'
at the cathedral.
Two drawings: Moses, dated
Dec. 28, 1897 and
Saint Olav, Oct. 13, 1899.

and every second be on the alert so there is no lapse, so nothing of one's personal technique sneaks in, nothing of one's personal, innermost feelings. Oh yes, that would be a lovely rest. Just the opposite; it would be consciously and violently tearing oneself up by the roots. If I were rich I would not bother to look at the cathedral. But I am poor, and therefore I m u s t s e l l p a r t o f w h a t i s i n s i d e m e.

In later life he looked back on this Trondheim period with mixed feelings. In 1921 he told his friend Aars: *Actually, I regret somewhat the time I spent there. I had to go against the grain, and work in a style.* A letter he wrote in 1923 contains these words, *It is impossible to work in a style which is not that of one's own time. The result is only a pastiche, no mattter how one looks at it.*

In Trondheim he worked in a miserable studio which had as one of its walls the cathedral wall itself. In the winter it was full of frost and ice, and there was no heating of any kind, with the result that his damp clay figures froze. Architect Christie had put a little trap-door leading from the floor of the

106

studio to the office underneath, and Vigeland later related: *Sometimes I had to stick my hands through that hole in the floor, and I can imagine that the people under me who had a nice warm stove, exulted when they saw my hands.*

In 1908 Vigeland wrote to the Ministry and asked to be relieved of the work at the cathedral. Liberated and light-hearted, he could then set to work on the great task which awaited him — *the Fountain.*

FREEDOM AND HARMONY

It has been said that Michelangelo, whom Vigeland admired above all others, never portrayed happiness. Vigeland, who was filled with great plans and had a number of commissions waiting, had literally freed himself from Christie's yoke. He felt himself a free man, and if he did not now depict actual happiness, he did have enough liberated energy to cultivate the more tender, emotional side of his nature. One might say that in *Mother and Child* from 1907 he portrayed happy devotion, if not actual happiness itself. The edgy, almost unbalanced works of his restless and struggling youth cede place, in this year of liberation, to a harmonious quality which this group exemplifies, and which is not to be found in his previous work.

Vigeland wrote a poem about the youthful years which were now behind him, and here he speaks of his *figures, linear, spare, gaunt / so like the self I was, so bony, sinewy / a tautness which I fashioned in ecstasy / yet thought came too late for my idea.* Thought, here, must mean the concept of form, of the finished work which infuses life into the idea. Now the time for thought had come, the time of ecstasy was past. Form now came into its own, and a sensation of happiness fills the form and interpenetrates the lines. A certain number of masterpieces from this period show that Vigeland had found a riper, quieter form than in his early works, one which is at the same time more disciplined than that of the later works.

In 1909, he carved in teak *Woman with Crossed Legs,* now in Norway's National Gallery. Here too, the same characteristics obtain. This harmonious, life-sized female figure reposing upon itself, speaks through its emotional content the same language as the *Mother and Child* group. The upper part in particular, with its pensively bowed head, radiates an indwelling harmonious beauty (p. 113).

An important factor in these years was the human warmth which surrounded Vigeland in daily life. The one work which

109

Torso, modelled in 1909, carved in marble in 1923.

is perhaps the most classical of all that he created came into being in 1909, and the model for it was the woman whose intimacy with the sculptor lasted for many years. Thus it is a portrait as well.

However, like all of us, the past was always present within him. He once said: *Making sketches is like putting money in the bank. I know I have them there and can 'withdraw' them whenever I need them.* During his whole life he jotted down ideas and motifs, no matter how vague or accidental they were.

110

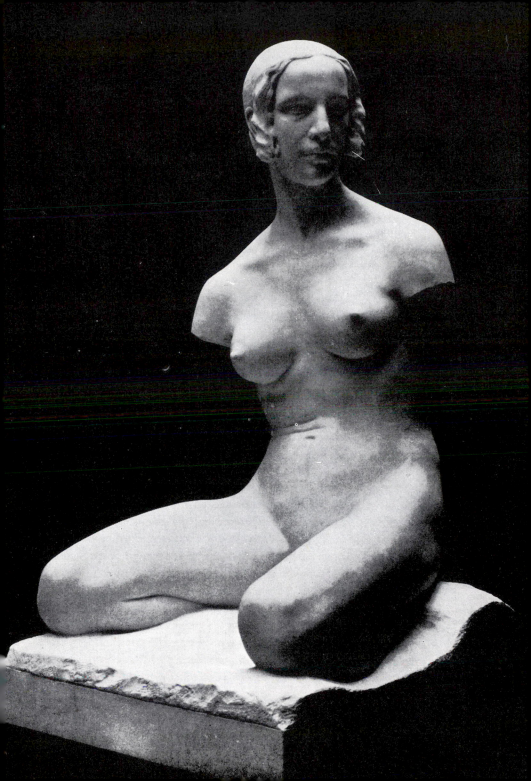

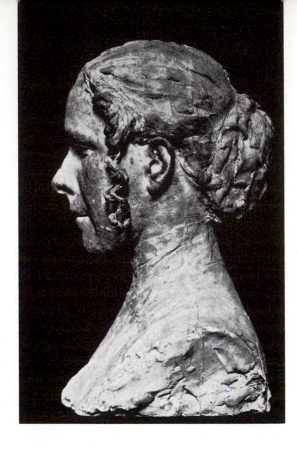

Inga Syvertsen, July 9, 1907, whose intimate relationship with the artist lasted for many years. P. 113: Woman with crossed legs, 1909, (detail).

He could pick up a sketch twenty years later and use it as a starting point for a large work. As we have already seen in the case of the commemorative statues, he dipped into his old sketches, taking up and transforming ideas and concepts which were often intended for other subjects. The extraordinarily rich period at the turn of the century when his imagination soared and ideas proliferated, was a well-spring upon which he drew until his death. This was only natural, as the one and only theme he treated was life — human life as we have all experienced it. Most people retain their inquisitiveness and openness to life as long as they feel young. Vigeland knew the importance of fresh ideas and a questioning attitude in both his private life and his art. *Making sketches keeps me young and*

Three plaster studies of Abel, Grieg and Bjørnson. P. 115: The Beggars, 1908. Erected in bronze at the Haukeland Hospital, Bergen.

supple inside, he said in later life. Sketching was his artistic rejuvenation.

For a sculptor a sketch need not be a drawing; it can also be a plastic study or rough model. Vigeland often drew upon his "bank." Thus it is that even in the harmonious period we are now considering, he could take up a study like *The Beggars* which dated from the nineties. He now did this group large-scale — more than six feet tall — making it into a monumental work. Here is evidence that the spirit pervading his first public success, *The Accursed,* and the influence of Auguste Rodin were still potent factors in his approach. The artist, who was then nearing 40, gave us one last outburst of the youth he was leaving behind and which lives on in the Fountain. In the years to come he was to travel farther and farther away from this style.

The plastic studies, like the drawings, often show signs of being spontaneous whims, simple jottings along the way, deposits

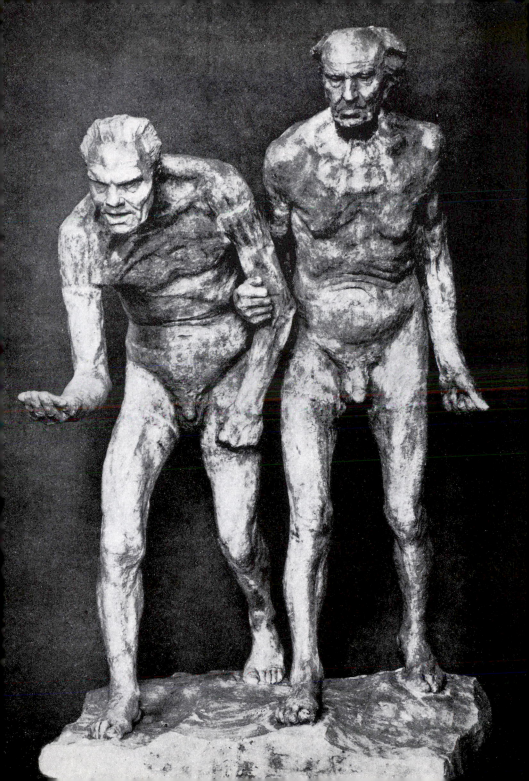

Bronze studies of Aasta Hansteen (1905), Petter Dass (1906) and Tordenskjold (1906).

in the bank he alluded to. Many of them could not possibly have been executed large-scale. The delightful, humorous sketch of the feminist *Aasta Hansteen*, with the umbrella which she used for chasing away heckling boys, was obviously not suitable for a large statue.

There are other pieces which, owing to their dramatic power, impress us deeply. One such is the magnificent preliminary study for a *Petter Dass* monument. It is regrettable that Vigeland never carried it beyond the study stage, for it might well have been one of the triumphs of Norwegian art.

However, there are dangers, and grave dangers at that, in the elderly Vigeland's views on the relationship between sketch

116

The artist installed in his new studio. 1923.

and finished work. He stated as late as 1939: *From the sketch to the finished work it is extremely rare for anything to be changed apart from the demands imposed by a large work.*

Here the master again has revealed what was precisely his weakness during the immense productivity of the latter years. Having moved into his new studio in 1923, and realizing that the time was approaching when his extensive plans would find fulfilment, he set about making numerous studies in the round with what we now call the Vigeland Park in mind. The fact that many of these studies came into being under the pressure of the enormous task Vigeland had set himself made such a procedure all the more hazardous. No one had forced this task upon him, but time was short.

117

The Fountain in the Frogner Sculpture Park.

THE FOUNTAIN
AND THE SCULPTURE PARK

As mentioned above, the idea behind Gustav Vigeland's main work, *The Fountain*, can be traced back to the eighteen-nineties. In 1900 he proposed to present the city of Oslo with a large group consisting of giants (then only four in number) who were to support a huge bowl. However, the offer was declined. Vigeland's reaction was to enlarge the plans, and during his travels in France in 1901 they took more definite shape. Originally Vigeland intended to surround the central bowl group with sixteen urn-like sculptures bearing human figures. Then one day, August 6, 1901 to be exact, the idea of a tree occurred to him, at first in connexion with a statue of Wergeland, as we have already seen (p. 49). The idea took root, and Vigeland made a number of drawings where Man and the Tree of Life are the recurring themes.

118

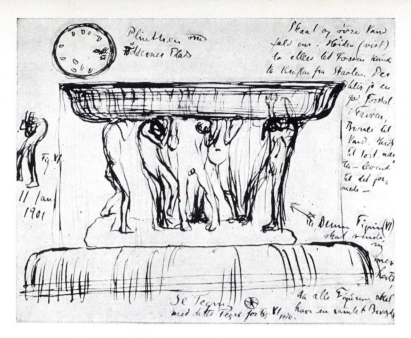

Drawing for the Giant Bowl, dated Jan. 11, 1901.

It was after seeing the early drawings of the giants' bowl and the surrounding urns in Paris in May 1901 that Gunnar Heiberg wrote his famous article, "The City with the Fountain." ...*With the Place de la Concorde in mind, I suddenly came to think of our own "Place" at home, stretching from the Parliament Building, which is neither beautiful nor even trim, but which has character and looks threatening to the (National) Theatre, which is so delightful inside ... I saw in my mind's eye the small helpless trees along our main street standing there gasping for air, looking as though they were given stones instead of earth to eat, and with only dogs to keep them watered. Parliament Place, which might be so lovely, and which could so easily be disfigured, especially if Norwegian-German architects are given free rein with decorative stairs and straight lines, with rocky cascades and turtles spouting water, with nymphs and gas-lights.*

Then I heard a voice at my ear: "Oh, to think if someone were allowed to make a beautiful square at home, no matter

Caricature by Olaf Gulbransson. Bjørnson reclining in the fountain as "the Nile." The bowl is held by prominent Norwegians of the period — Bætzmann, Lie, Grieg, Ibsen and Nansen. The little figures are also well-known personalities such as Nærup, Thomas and Vilhelm Krag.

how small it might be." It was a western dialect, with soft consonants. I recognized the voice. It belongs to a great artist, the only titanic one of all those who have lived and who now live among us.

"I want to have six nude male figures lifting a bowl high above their heads. Different men, all of them naked: happy and serious, young and old, and water would pour out of the bowl — nothing more. It would be lovely, I think, in the three-cornered place by the Parliament ... Or just imagine, if I could do what I would like to do more than anything else in the world," — I remember the fire in his eyes — "right in the middle of Parliament Place, a pool, about' 150 feet across, a low barrier around it, in the middle of the pool eight — then

*there would have to be eight — naked men, but they would
have to be four or five times natural size, towering against
the sky, and around the pool just on the edge there would be
sixteen urns six feet high — sixteen! — all with the same
basic form, but each of them different from the others, and
on each of these there would be figures of normal size — think
if I could get to do that. That, I believe, is the greatest thing
I could ever do in my whole life."*

*And I remember the drawings he showed me for the urns
and the people on them, not in high relief, but statues, young
women standing up, men climbing, little boys playing around
the top of the urns — a world of bodies stretching and twisting,
strength and grace, violence and quiet reflection, everything a
great sculptor's fantasy, feelings and understanding find in
the human body and give back to us as living art which in its
turn gives birth to imaginativeness and a sense of beauty and
love of line and respect for the naked body.*

121

And I thought: That would be something for all the citizens of Oslo who have ambitions for their city, and want to make it a big city and a great city, if ever the day should come when Norway's capital is known the world over as "the City with the fountain."

Gunnar Heiberg was not alone in his efforts to turn Vigeland's fountain into a reality. Jens Thiis gave a number of lectures on the subject, and his book, "Norwegian Painters and Sculptors", (1905) closes with a homage to Vigeland. Its concluding words are: *Will this hymn to life ever resound in bronze and stone under the open sky, or will it die within the confines of the studio? Will t h e   c i t y   w i t h   t h e   F o u n - t a i n become a reality?*

In 1906 the Swedish art critic Tor Hedberg published an enthusiastic article on Vigeland in Sweden. It concludes thus: *He is already a great artist — I should like to shout it so loudly that it could be heard as far as Norway, and that in his own country room would be found for his work.*

In 1906 a model of the fountain, one fifth its final size, was put on display at the Museum of Applied Art in Oslo. It aroused enormous interest and enthusiasm. However, it would have been extraordinary if such a deeply personal, daring and modern work as the Fountain did not provoke opposition. The painter Christian Krohg had previously done all he could to prevent the erection of the Abel monument. He had written highly irrelevant articles in which, among other things, he likened Abel to a jockey riding two horses. Where the Fountain was concerned (and he had only seen pictures of studies of both Abel and the Fountain), Krohg ridiculed it by comparing it to a punch bowl surrounded by long-stemmed glasses. He got a well-deserved reply from the author Nils Kjær, one of Norway's finest prose stylists, who put Christian Krohg forcefully in his place with a caustic and witty article of rebuttal:

Model of the Fountain, exhibited in Oslo's Museum of Applied Art, 1906.

It is not impossible that Christian Krohg has a fertile imagination, and that this imagination as he himself says, is a radius. If this is the case, this radius measures the distance between the centre of his intelligence and the outermost periphery of absurdity, to which it extends each time he comes into proximity with Vigeland's art ... Krohg had asked how the water was to get up to the giants' bowl. Nils Kjær answers him, asking how it has got into all the lions' mouths of all the fountains in the world. He also wonders if Krohg has never asked himself where that little manikin in Brussels gets all his water from ... He concludes: *If I should some day see a statue of Christian Krohg showing him holding a bowl or a bucket or some other household article high above his head, and with water cascading down over his shoulders, I would not make any smallish or contentious objections. I would probably be content to assume that the work adequately expressed its content, and I would say to myself: Why if it isn't Christian Krohg, above his ears in water!*

Among certain sculptors as well, there was some lively intrigue. Talk went round about "the by-passing of other sculptors," and it was suggested that a competition be held to

Ernest Thiel, Swedish financier who befriended Vigeland on several occasions.
P. 125: "The Swallow," tree-group from the Fountain in Frogner Park.

select a fountain for the Studenterlund gardens. One of the conservative newspapers published an article by the official state architect complaining about the *six heavily-laden men who are to confront our hard climate in Adam's costume ... Inquiries have been made in vain as to just what sort of events will be depicted in the many, many reliefs in the high walls around the pool.*

A rumour was circulated that Vigeland's health would not permit him to live long enough to complete the work. Whereupon he obtained certificates of health from three prominent physicians to the effect that there was nothing whatsoever the matter with him.

Vigeland and his fountain became a cherished theme of the humorous magazines. He received streams of anonymous letters, yet he took all the opposition calmly, and was quoted in an interview as saying, *"These attacks are excellent; they have*

been of more service than most of the positive articles which have been written."

The Minister of Finance, the Minister of Education and members of Parliament were asked their opinion, and they came to Vigeland's defence, some of them also making concrete proposals for solving the financial side of the problem. A number of prominent men and women promised to give their support.

Just how great public interest was can be seen from an article written by the editor of one of Oslo's leading newpapers: *The masses of people which streamed past the model yesterday may have understood in varying degrees what they saw, but there was hardly one who did not have a solemn feeling of being confronted with something great and remarkable. It is no exaggeration to say that we are dealing here with one of the largest works of art ever to be executed in Norway by one man.* Then there follows an appeal for funds. *Here at*

126

last we have the opportunity to erect as fine a monument as Norway is capable of.

It happened that no less than 4,000 people came, in the course of one single day, to see the model. The Swedish art critic and collector, Klas Fåhræus, recorded the impression made on him by the visitors and their reactions: *One felt that one stood facing an accomplishment which, in the realm of art, verged on the miraculous. I imagine it was in a similar frame of mind that the faithful consecrated their cathedrals in the devout Middle Ages.*

The numerous pilgrim-like visitors were not the only ones who were moved to make a contribution. Patrons of the arts also demonstrated their interest. Klas Fåhræus, cited above, made a contribution. Ernst Thiel, a Swedish banker and founder of Stockholm's Thielska Gallery, sent a cheque for 50,000 crowns. This was a magnificent gesture on the part of a Swede, considering that this was just two years after Norway had severed all ties with Sweden. But this gesture had a threat attached to it, for Thiel declared that if the city of Oslo did not carry out Vigeland's plans, it would give him the greatest pleasure to have the fountain erected in Stockholm. Vigeland replied that as far as he was concerned all that mattered was for his project to become a reality, so at one time it looked as though the whole fountain might travel across the border!

However, the citizens of Oslo met the challenge and money was raised. The cost of the fountain was estimated at 250,000 Norwegian crowns — a sum which then seemed deliriously fantastic. Nevertheless within a matter of months this amount was collected, partly by means of private subscriptions, partly through funds which the city of Oslo made available.

The model which Vigeland put on display in 1906 differed somewhat from the final version. The basic plan was not quadratic as it later became, but was more organic in form, curving in and out in the art nouveau style. The tree-groups were not bunched together at the four corners of the pool as is now the case, but were spread out along its sides so that they stood out better. The urns were to hold living plants. *From the urns flowers and creeping plants will wave to us in the summertime, and in winter upon important occasions torches will blaze from them. And it will all grow more and more lovely with the years! The time will come when its metal will blaze green and resplendent under our smoke-filled sky, telling our great-grandchildren that artists have existed in this land of ours.* (Excerpt from a newspaper article which appeared in 1906.)

The twenty bronze trees framing the fountain are Vigeland's synthesis of everything which occupied his spirit. They grew out of an exuberantly prolific imagination and a deep humility towards life. First there is the Tree of Life where tiny dormant children swarm "like a clump of bees," as Vigeland said of them. Then there is the young boy who has awakened to life

The tree-groups on these and the preceding pages were modelled in the years from 1907 to 1914. They trace all of life's phases, from the cradle to the grave.

and who looks around him in astonishment. "Self-portrait from boyhood," Vigeland wrote on a drawing for this second group. The boy meets a friend and they climb the tree together. This group may have been inspired by boys stealing apples, but in any case Vigeland situates the motif on a higher plane, permitting us to regard this group in a larger philosophic perspective. Here we meet the same idea Edvard Munch treated in that part of his Aula murals called "The Explorers." Vigeland shows the boys investigating this remarkable tree they are climbing. They are eager for knowledge in their exploration of the tree-top, whereas the little girls in the next group are not so active. These three charming little graces stand beneath the tree and whisper their secrets. They may be whispering about a friend, the girl in the fifth tree-group who is plunging into life. She hurtles through the Tree of Life like a swallow, and in fact her creator always referred to this group as "The

Swallow." She does not know where she will land, and her whole body expresses terror. Her arms are pressed close to her breast, her hands are clenched in anxiety, while her eyes are wide open and her lips parted. There is the same air about her as that we find in the painting by Munch called "Puberty."

In the succeeding groups Vigeland continued his portrayals of youth. It may be the same girl we now meet a few years later as a grown woman. She leans out of the tree, all peaceful contemplation — waiting. Then we see her encounter with a man in the shadow of the tree's foliage. Vigeland goes on to show us loneliness, love and disappointment. His presentations of man's and woman's respective reveries have great poignancy, but they are very different. The man is standing, his gaze directed outward, as he dreams of what he is going to accomplish in life. Or perhaps he is listening to the voice of inspiration, as was the poet Wergeland in the first sketch based on this theme. Vigeland called this tree-group "The Spirit of Wergeland," whereas he titled the next group "Woman on an

131

Animal." The woman is seated on the trunk of the tree, and this trunk resembles an animal in shape. Vigeland provided it with a tail, hind-legs and fore-legs, and up in the leaves he gave it a semblance of a head. He may have had the idea from an ancient olive tree he once sketched in Florence. This representation of a woman and a tree can be interpreted however, as one of the aspects of a more penetrating description of the relationship between man and woman. *The man* looks forward, beyond the tree, dreaming of the great things he will achieve. *The woman*, eyes shut, is seated on the tree-trunk, enclosed within herself, with her arm round the trunk which is almost a living creature. It is likely that she may simply be thinking of the little child sitting lost and alone in the Tree of Life, sucking its thumb.

Vigeland's pessimistic outlook is expressed in the succeeding group. Here we find a man and a woman closely entwined, yet struggling to get free of one another. They struggle in vain, for the Tree of Life has become a living creature and has intervened in their lives. The branches twist round them and prevent them from breaking apart. Then there is the man who is swinging through the Tree of Life, and another who chases life away from him. Life, here, is symbolized by tiny weeping creatures who seek shelter in the top of the tree, frightened by the man's enraged gestures.

In the last five groups Vigeland portrays old age. There is the old man who clings to the tree. There is the touching old grandmother whose aged body would normally be called repulsive, but who possesses a certain beauty because she is the expression of an uncompromising truthfulness and a profound humanity. Then there is the grandfather telling a tale to a little boy. Here again we are made to think of Munch's Aula murals — this time of the panel called "History." The next to the last group shows us a man who does not want to die and who clutches at the tree, shouting a hysterical No! But to no avail. In the twentieth and last group Death has placed

Detail of the tree-group, Old Woman and Little Child, 1908.

Reliefs from wall of pool. Young boy and girl, 1913. Three boys. 1912–14.

itself in the Tree of Life. Vigeland purposely treated Death's skeleton body and the tree's branches in the same way. There is hardly any difference between them. The skeleton's feet are placed so as to suggest the return of energy, via the trunk of life's tree, to the earth we have come from.

The sixty reliefs on the walls of the pool provide an accompaniment to the tree-groups. The themes are similar, but there being sixty reliefs and only twenty trees, a greater number of subjects can be presented. The first relief shows the past as it crumbles away, symbolized by a large skull of a prehistoric animal. On the horn of the skull we see the future standing, represented by a tiny being. In the next relief preparations are being made for the arrival of life as more of these tiny creatures take up the skulls and bones. They fly away and are replaced by real children who play with animals, pulling the wolf's tail and sticking their arms deep into its mouth. Then there are children approaching puberty — a group of boys

134

Reliefs. Woman and Unicorn, 1906. Old man discoursing to two boys. 1930–35.

with their backs to the adult world. Are they absorbed by their first cigarette, some unusual stone they have found, or perhaps a four-letter word scrawled on a wall? It is certainly something secret, whatever it may be.

There is a young boy meeting his girl for the first time. We can follow their difficulties as they turn their backs to each other, and the mother scolds her young daughter. We see a man erect, lost in thought among little genii, and a woman seated in the horns of a reindeer. There is a boy who lies dreaming, with a voluptuous woman floating above him, and there is a woman giving her breast to a unicorn. Can the unicorn symbolize man liberated from the animal kingdom by woman's love? We see a woman between two men, and a man between a young girl and a mature woman. Then there is a couple engaged in the dance of life, and another couple floating upwards as in a dream, the woman's hair twining around the man's throat.

135

Queue in front of Vigeland's old studio, 1916.

Farther on Vigeland speaks of old age — of the lonely old hypocrite who is afraid to die, of death itself separating two lovers, of people falling down, becoming skeletons and crumbling away in the great void. It is from this void, however, that the cranium emerges in the first relief, and standing on it there is the symbol of the future and of continuing life. The cycle has come full turn — life begins anew.

In April of 1916 Vigeland opened his studio to the public. Normally, it was not easy to gain access there. It was no wonder that the ordinary visitor was captivated by what he saw upon entering the workshop of the master and the idyllic little garden where the completed bronze tree-groups stood. For three days on end a queue of silent, fascinated spectators

136

Bronze tree-groups and granite groups in the garden of the old studio, November 1919.

inched its way past Vigeland's work. When the visitors had seen all there was to see they ran back and queued up again.

The Fountain is Vigeland's "frieze of life," a counterpart to the series of paintings by Edvard Munch which was called, in fact, "Frieze of Life," and a number of the Fountain's themes are closely related to Munch's work. Here then ordinary people encountered an artist with a message to communicate to his fellow-men, and who spoke in a language which was simple and could be readily understood.

Yet, in spite of the obvious impression Vigeland's art had made on the citizenry of Oslo, there were still those who opposed the artist and his far-reaching plans. Certain of his opponents could hardly be taken seriously, as for instance the

137

clergyman who wrote in a religious weekly magazine, claiming that *the Fountain will have a demoralizing effect. The project as a whole is far removed from the spirit of Christianity . . . If we keep silent now, what will we answer before God's judgment seat?* He went so far as to call it "an open-air temple to Astarte." His reactions to what he felt was Vigeland's paganism were much the same as those the Catholic author Evelyn Waugh was later to express in the same connexion.

There were others however, whose criticisms were better founded. The art critic Jappe Nilssen, for example, feared that Vigeland's plans would assume such dimensions that they would get out of hand. Vigeland had, in fact, evolved a new scheme. He proposed to place the fountain along the driveway leading to the Royal Palace. Jappe Nilssen commented: *This time it is the Abel Hill (in front of the Palace). Next time he*

P. 138: Scale-model for proposed Fountain-complex on Abel Hill. Ca. 1917.
This page: The artist outside his studio, circa 1920.

may take it into his head to refashion the entire Palace Park. Vigeland is a great artist, a man of genius whom all of us deeply respect, yet not so deeply that we can go along with all of his projects.

The misgivings of his opponents are easy to understand, for Vigeland's plan was truly gigantic. The fountain, its bronze tree-groups now completed, was to be placed on the hill where Vigeland's Abel monument was standing. The plateau on top of the hill was to be paved with an enormous labyrinth of grey and black granite, differing somewhat from the labyrinth now found in the Sculpture Park. On the encompassing balustrade there were to be large stone lanterns. A middle plateau was to be populated by 28 granite groups and dragon-like figures almost ten feet tall. A huge semi-circular staircase was to be ornamented with 38 large granite groups. There were also to be granite groups facing a path traversing the park. The

139

Vigeland in his
studio.
P. 141: A corner
of the studio.

actual approach to the Palace was to be flanked by large
groups showing humans struggling with dragon-like creatures
— rather an unusual entryway for a royal palace! All in all,
the plans included 99 large granite groups, in addition to the
fountain complex!

A note Vigeland made in 1915 shows how the plans
gradually overpowered the artist. *In the first plan I kept the
trees and the surrounding streets in mind. In the second plan
I had less regard for the trees, but still took the streets into
consideration. In the third and final plan I took nothing
whatsoever into consideration.*

Although there were those like Jappe Nilssen who had
their doubts, the reactions voiced when these plans were first
presented were surprising, for on the whole the project was
given a very positive reception. To aid in financing the work
an expensive publication was brought out, containing articles
by many Norwegian art critics and public personalities.

A new committee was formed to collect money for the cutting of the granite groups. One ship-owner promised to contribute a million Norwegian crowns, and another 175,000 crowns was collected through private subscriptions.

Vigeland needed a large and better studio if these dreams were to come to life. Even though the municipality had rebuilt his old studio in 1908, it was still far too small. There were shelves from floor to ceiling filled with studies waiting to be done large-scale, and the garden was full of bronze trees and recent granite groups.

Thus it was that the idea occurred to Vigeland to write the authorities and simply offer them all his works on the condition that they would build him a studio large enough to enable him to bring to life the projects he and many others with him had dreamt of for so long. He telephoned Aars, the city archi-

141

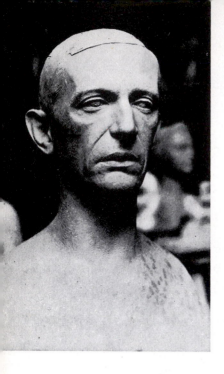

The municipal architect, Harald Aars. January 30, 1922. Study for the Monolith, spring 1919. P. 143: Three sketches for the Monolith.

tect, and read him the letter he planned to send the Ministry of Education. Aars asked him to wait a minute, hurried to the studio and persuaded Vigeland to re-address the letter. Thus it was sent not to the State, but to the city of Oslo, and the unexpected happened, for the municipality replied in the affirmative. This is what led up to the signing, in 1921, of the most remarkable contract ever made between an artist and a public body. Gustav Vigeland presented all he had made and everything he would thereafter make to the city of Oslo. He also turned his extensive library over to the city, in addition to the ownership rights to his entire production. He could continue to execute and sell commissioned works, but the municipality retained the rights to all original models. In return the city was to build Vigeland a studio complete with living quarters, and after his death it would become his museum.

Vigeland had no thought of selling his works to the city. He did not want it to be said that he had grown rich on the

contract. What he did gain was of greater importance to an artist than money, for he was given working conditions the like of which no other artist has had.

Such circumstances were unparalleled in the history of art. For the first time an artist was altogether free to create whatever he wished without regard to his patron. What would Michelangelo, whom Vigeland admired more than any other sculptor, not have given for such a privilege, not to mention Phidias? Vigeland was absolutely unrestricted. He could make whatever he liked, content in the knowledge that it would be carefully preserved. He was given all the technical help he required. All the practical difficulties a sculptor is faced with — costly materials, expensive help, lack of space — were eliminated at one stroke. It was decided to build him both a studio and living quarters, and after the artist's death the building was to serve as his mausoleum and museum.

Vigeland moved into the completed part of his studio in 1923. The preceding year he had sought permission to erect

Detail of
the Monolith.
P. 145:
The Monolith and
some of its 36
surrounding granite
groups.

his sculpture complex on the area in front of the studio. A
new work, "The Human Pillar," had come into being as the
crowning element of the whole project. However, some of his
warmest supporters felt that the space in front of the studio was
an unsatisfactory location and asked the artist to choose another.
In 1924, after some discussion, the City Council approved Vigeland's plan for the sculpture complex in Frogner Park, with the
Monolith to be erected atop a small hill.

Three years later the great 260-ton block of stone was set
in place. A structure with internal stairs was built around it.
The plaster sections of the model were put together, making
a column more than 55 ft. high. The cutting commenced, and
when on August 20, 1943, the scaffolding was removed, the
public had its first view of the completed Monolith.

Vigeland had made many sketches preparatory to this
human pillar. The first of these studies had the column supported
by dragons which coiled round it like a band. Dragons and

mythical beasts still haunted his imagination to the extent that he made one sketch in which the Monolith consisted entirely of such creatures.

The finished work consists of 121 interlacing human bodies. They mount in an ever-increasing crescendo towards the summit where young women, girls and children rise towards the light, the sun, towards the sphere of ideals. "Let each interpret it as he likes." Vigeland once replied when asked just what the Monolith 'meant.' "It is my religion," he said on another occasion. At the time when the City Council was debating whether or not to erect the Monolith Vigeland stated, "If they vote against the monolith they might just as well vote to decide who is going to murder me."

In this period Vigeland also evolved a plan for replacing the bridge in Frogner Park which had served for the 1914

146

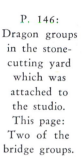

P. 146:
Dragon groups
in the stone-
cutting yard
which was
attached to
the studio.
This page:
Two of the
bridge groups.

centenary celebration of Norway's independence. His first plan for a stone bridge with railings made up of intertwining dragons. Large dragons and mythical beasts similar to those of earlier plans were to ornament the bridge. However, he eventually discarded the idea, and only the four tall dragon groups, two at each end of the bridge, were executed. There are in existence studies in the round for many more groups of this kind, for the dragon motif was one which never ceased to interest the sculptor.

Vigeland finally decided on a bridge bearing bronze statues. With breath-taking speed he turned out no less than 58 large bronze figures, the theme once again being life in all its phases. Below the bridge he designed a small circular area, placing an unborn baby upside down in the centre, and surrounding it by eight tiny children at play.

In 1930 Vigeland opened his studio to the public for the second time. The interest aroused was perhaps even greater than in 1916. During the 28 days the studio was open it was visited by 74,000 people, making an average of about 2,700

147

The embrace; Father, mother
and child: Two granite groups
from the Monolith plateau,
both 1917.
Below: Little girl from the
bridge, and unborn child from
the children's area.
P. 149: The Wheel of Life, 1934.

148

visitors per day. This was the first time the model of the 100-metre long bridge with its 58 statues was put on display. At the last meeting of the City Council before the 1931 summer holidays Vigeland's plans for the bridge were approved.

The public debate, however, was in full swing. Protests were voiced, with varying degrees of objectivity, from many sides. The discussion, which was primitive in the extreme, will be taken up in the next chapter.

Gate at Kirkeveien entrance to Frogner Park.
P. 151: Three women walking. Gate on Monolith plateau.

Vigeland died in 1943, but it was not until 1950 that his *Wheel of Life* was erected in Frogner Park. Later on certain smaller works, plus the base of his sun-dial were added.

Vigeland had planned to enclose the whole area by means of eleven large bronze gates, but only the monumental entrance gates were erected. There are many imaginative details in their wrought iron artisanry, but the large and unique wrought iron gates framing the Monolith's plateau are more beautiful by far.

In these pages we have drawn the main contours of Gustav Vigeland's prodigious oeuvre and the debate it aroused during the artist's life. The Sculpture Park caused difficulties in Vigeland's relationships with his friends, and it created problems for himself as an artist. Its history, starting from the initial concept, stretches over half a century, and during this period the times changed, as did the artist.

The gentle, curvate lines appropriate to art nouveau could not survive in a gigantic sculpture complex where the T-square presided. Thus it was that Vigeland traced a severely perfect circle around the Monolith.

Unfortunately, it was the bridge which gave the public its first impression of the Sculpture Park, for the first part of the complex to be erected was this gargantuan structure, peopled with large bronze groups, spanning only a little stream. Even though it was designed last, the bridge no longer spoke the idiom of the day. In this way the final phase of the Vigeland debate got off to a wrong start, and the discussion still rages on. Nor should it come to an end, for all vital art has always stirred up discord.

In this little book as well, the discussion must be continued, for in the next chapter we turn to Vigeland's problems and The Vigeland Problem.

P. 153: Man struggling against
a monster.

This page: Vigeland's death mask. P. 155: Gustav Vigeland in 1891, by Ludvig Brandstrup. Vigeland's self-portrait, Jan. 16—19, 1922.

ON VIGELAND'S PROBLEMS AND THE VIGELAND PROBLEM

There are three sculptural portraits of Gustav Vigeland in existence. The earliest is a bust made by a Danish friend, Ludvig Brandstrup, who studied together with Vigeland under C. V. Bissen. It shows Vigeland as a 22-year old. The second is a self-portrait done at the age of 52, after the studio contract was signed. The third is a full-length portrait statue which Vigeland made in 1942, the year before his death, and which he had intended to place at the entrance of the Frogner Sculpture Park. In addition to these there is the artist's death mask.

By examining these portraits we may be able to learn something more about their subject. When comparing Brandstrup's bust with Vigeland's self-portrait bust it is hard to realize that they depict the same person. They are, of course, a generation apart, and allowance must also be made for the differences between the two artists who created them. On

the other hand, if we compare each of the busts with photographs taken at the respective periods, we find that they are both striking likenesses. Moreover, in comparing Brandstrup's bust with a bust Vigeland did of his brother Emanuel, then also in his early twenties, we can observe a true family likeness.

The change which occurred in these thirty years is so drastic that one necessarily wonders just what happened to the man Gustav Vigeland.

The youth we see in Brandstrup's bust is thin, almost ascetic in appearance. The head juts weakly forward and is held to one side above a long slender neck whose Adam's

Hans Dedekam,
Sept. 3, 1923.
Mrs. Ingerid
Vigeland, 1922.
P. 157:
The artist and
his wife amid
greetings from
well-wishers.

apple is very much in evidence. The hair is unruly and unkempt. The cheekbones protrude markedly from the thin face, and yet the features are soft. The lips are full and the chin is slightly weak (in this it resembles Vigeland's bust of his brother Emanuel). Brandstrup demonstrated a perceptive eye and a sensitive hand in shaping the features of his friend.

At one stage of his early career Vigeland modelled his own portrait (p. 9). The bust no longer exists, but there is a photograph which shows both it and its creator. Much of the same softness and weakness can be seen in this bust. Unfortunately Vigeland tore it down as he was in need of clay for other works. Afterwards, Vigeland showed no desire whatsoever to portray himself. He once remarked to a friend that "all self-portraits are worthless as character portrayals — they show only trappings, theatre and posturing." In 1922 he did a self-portrait nonetheless, though just prior to doing so he had said, "all self-portraits idealize. No artist has ever depicted himself as ugly or evil."

156

Turning to this bust we find a facial expression that is stern, reserved and almost intimidating. In his desperate attempt not to expose himself we find something that is at once mask-like and unpleasantly revealing. The artist has refused to penetrate behind outer appearances, in contrast to so many of the other portraits he had done. We are reminded of his own words, "I am my worst friend; I am my best enemy."

The bust faces squarely front. The hair is smoothly combed and follows the contours of the powerful head. The once long and slender neck has become short and thick. The youthful softness of the features is now replaced by a strained expression, with furrowed brow and a tightly shut mouth. The mouth was doubtless intended to express forcefulness and decisiveness, but it reveals suspiciousness and even vexation. The massive chin is worthy of an emperor.

Again we wonder what has happened. This bust was modelled at the very moment when all of the artist's greatest hopes had materialized. The contract was signed. The studio was in

157

construction. Vigeland had recently married and his young wife brought new happiness into his life, for as he said to his friends, *"Marriage is the only thing. Nothing else counts."* Or again, *"One of the few sensible things I have done was to marry my present wife."* All in all, no artist before him was ever privileged with such ideal working conditions.

If we wish to form an idea of some of the factors contributing to the change in the artist we need not depend on subjective judgments but can turn to two main sources. The first consists of Vigeland's own words — his letters and the notes he made on his problems, personal as well as artistic. The second group of sources is of another type. Vigeland is one of the fortunate few who were like Johnson in having a Boswell. In fact he had several such friends who admired him and were intimate with him. Two of them kept records of many of Vigeland's remarks as material for books they intended to write. One was a museum director, Hans Dedekam, whose collection of Vigeland statements, "Notes from Visits at

P. 158: Petter Dass riding to Copenhagen on the devil's back. Woodcut.
This page: Ingerid Vilberg, 1921, later Mrs. Vigeland.

Self-portrait in
smock, June 6, 1942.
P. 162: Man and
woman, 1908.

Vigeland's Studio," can be found in manuscript form in the
Vigeland Museum (Vigeland himself approved the manu-
script). The other was the municipal architect, Harald Aars.
Excerpts from his diary were published in 1951 by Karl Just.

In a note dating from 1902 Vigeland wrote: *When a painter
or sculptor talks about what he intends to do you must never
for a moment think that the finshed work will be anything like
the impression of it which you got from his description.
Remember that while he is 'carrying out' the work faculties
are set in motion that are quite different from those which
help him to describe it.* Vigeland is surely right. Nevertheless,
an artist's own words about his problems will always be of
interest. Therefore, in what is to follow, constant reference will
be made to all three sources mentioned above.

We have already cited certain of Vigeland's writings con-
cerning his childhood and youth, his father's strict puritanism
and the feeling of always carrying his childhood with him.
There can be no doubt that the unfortunate circumstances in
his childhood home marked him deeply, characterized as they

160

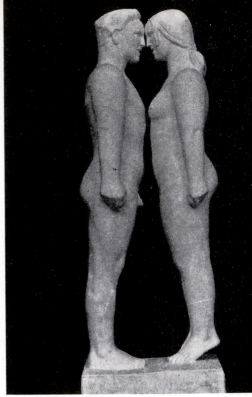

were by illness and death, by stern religiosity and by threats of hellfire and damnation.

Young Gustav tried to escape into a world of his own. He was an introverted child who read much and drew even more. Later he was to write of this period as follows: *I knew Greek and Roman mythology, and could recite long passages from the Iliad and the Odyssey. I thought the Greeks were more beautiful and better people than those I read about in the Bible. I hated the Bible's words about not making any graven images, and I hated too when people called sculpture graven images, and when they said that violin music and sculpture belonged to the Devil. "Why, that's an idol!" said one Bible-brandishing fundamentalist of a little figure I had made. Iconoclasts were murderers in my eyes. It was as though my brother Theodor and I were heading straight for Hell.*

162

P. 162:
Man and Woman, 1898.
Man and Woman, 1939.
This page:
Man in the grip of a tree,
1900. A dream Vigeland
had had.

In 1922 he said to his friend Dedekam: *West Norwegian puritanism contains a vast fund of emotion. When it is turned in another direction, when it follows another course, then it has enormous power and can accomplish great things. Eastern Norway has materialism instead of puritanism.*

We have seen in the foregoing how in his youth Vigeland revolved constantly around the same subjects — sorrow, repentance, doubt and remorse. He once told Dedekam, *There has only been a sprinkling of joy in my life. It has found only small expression in my art.* Dedekam remarked: *What he lost as a person served to enrich his art. He would have liked to be like the others and capture joy. But he could not. He was in good company however — Michelangelo, Dante, Beethoven, Æschylus — who was like an earthquake.*

163

Eros and Psyche, 1898.
P. 165: Man holding a woman in his arms, 1905.

Vigeland did not hesitate to compare himself with the truly great. He was never lacking in self-assurance. As early as 1896 he had written, *Not that I want to be understood, oh no. I do not work for people at all, no, for I shall be a factor in future 'developments' in any case.*

Aars, the architect, once tried to persuade Vigeland to send some photographs of his work to the German art historian Albert Dresdner, who was hoping to write something about Vigeland. Aars argued that Vigeland did not have the renown in Europe to which he was entitled. Vigeland countered by saying, "I don't need it; I am in no hurry, I can wait. I know very well what my works are worth, for I am acquainted

164

Gustav Vigeland, 1918.
P. 167: Model of the bridge,
1930.

with most of the world's sculpture." As for Albert Dresdner, Vigeland declared, "Let him write first so I can see where I have him. Let Europe come here!"

Nor could Professor Schnitler of Oslo University persuade Vigeland to exhibit some of his works in 1917. Vigeland recorded his reactions to the proposal: *Exhibiting the large stone groups would be idiotic. Sending monumental works on a jaunt round about is undignified; let Europe come up and see them when they have been erected here. Did "the ancients" send their works on tour? Were the pyramids and the Indian cliff temples trundled around Europe? I for one have never bothered much with exhibitions. But to get some peace at last and to put an end to all the pestering and clamouring for an exhibition I opened my studio and let people go through it for nearly a month without removing even the smallest or most insignificant thing. Apart from the purely artistic side, I would say a more honest exhibition has never been held.*

166

There are two exhibitions which I am interested in. There is the one I visualize in which my works are arranged in rooms befitting them, on view for posterity, and owned by the state or the city. The other is the one on Abel Hill.

The fact of Vigeland's abundant self-assurance need not surprise us. Professor Dietrichson had applied the word genius to Vigeland when he was still a youth. Bjørnson proclaimed it to the nation. We have seen how many of Norway's keenest and most critical writers spoke of him in superlatives. At the age of 26 a panegyric book was written about him by a member of the circle of artists and litterati in which Vigeland moved. At the time of the Fountain debate the newspapers carried column after column of discussion. As his plans grew more extensive there were of course those who protested, but the throngs of Vigeland's admirers always outnumbered them.

Contemporary art has always bred controversy and ought always to do so, provided it has something to say to the world.

167

The discussion arising from Gustav Vigeland's art, however, was unusually muddled and confused. Opinion was sharply divided. Abuse was countered with praise, blind admiration with execration. Objective and unobjective arguments were intermingled to such an extent that the whole controversy grew chaotic. Personal dislikes and professional jealousies were allowed to influence opinions. Moreover there were all those who tended to run with the herd, slaves of jargon and the current fads.

It was only natural for criticism to be voiced when one single artist was awarded such excellent working conditions and others, like Munch, got nothing. Young Norwegian sculptors felt they were being by-passed, and there were many with hurt feelings.

It is a fact that Vigeland would not accept good advice. As we have mentioned above there were those, like the municipal architect, who tried to prevent Vigeland's plans from getting out of hand. They were removed from the committees concerned, and Vigeland then proceeded with his projects. At one point it was suggested that Vigeland work together with an architect. The whole idea was inconceivable to him, and his only response was a laconic "Two mothers cannot give birth to one child." He closed the doors of his studio and allowed only a few people in. General irritation with him mounted. The press were annoyed, and though few had actually seen the work in progress, there were many who wrote articles as if they had. An atmosphere of irrational animosity developed.

When the time came to set up the works in Frogner Park the mistake was made of erecting the bridge and its figures first. The bridge is one of Vigeland's later and weaker works, and it immediately put wind into the sails of his opponents. The turbulent controversy continued. When the Fountain was erected it also was criticized. More than a generation had elapsed since the young Vigeland had fashioned this epic poem

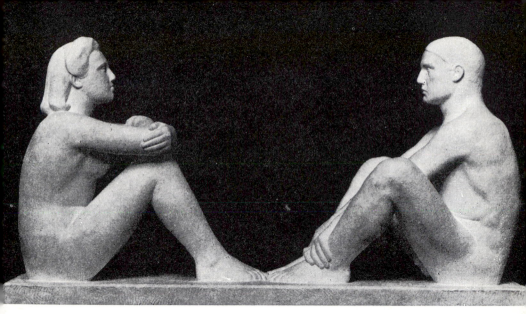

Above: Man and woman, seated. Group (1941), intended for a projected bridge in Frogner Park (not erected).

Below: Groups in clay, plaster, bronze and granite in the artist's studio.

of life, and now it was to be judged by the down-to-earth functionalists of the 1930's.

Above all it was Vigeland the architect who was criticized, and rightly so. As the years passed he grew more and more dependent on his T-square. The fountain's curvilinear ground-plan was replaced by a sober "functional" rectangle which did not harmonize with the art nouveau style of the tree-groups. Straight walks were imposed on the gently rolling terrain, and blocks of terraces rose one above the other.

Again the newspapers were filled with the debate. There were torrents of abuse, with opinions becoming increasingly partisan. People thought they were discussing Vigeland's art, but they were only discussing the bridge, the bastion of terraces and the Monolith or, as it was called, "the phallic symbol." No one thought of considering Vigeland's production in its entirety. No serious attempt has yet been made to view his work in relation to the rest of Norwegian sculpture or to European sculpture as a whole. Vigeland would doubtless profit by such a comparison.

P. 170: Girl on a reindeer, October 1920. Girl on a bear, bronze, 1921. Freia Park, Oslo. This page:
Man struggling against a monster. Woodcut.

Since the 1947 opening of the studio turned museum, the rudimentary views described above have gradually given way to more nuanced appraisals. The works of Vigeland's younger years, which had been almost totally forgotten in the heat of the battle, were put on display. The commemorative statues and portrait busts were there for all to see, and Vigeland gradually regained some of the position he had once had.

It must be pointed out that the controversy centering upon Vigeland was not of the kind which normally surrounds an artist's work, the reason being that during his lifetime he had already been publicly labelled 'genius.' There may be more hazards attached to receiving such official sanction when alive than after one is dead and history passes judgment. Being placed on Mount Parnassus during one's lifetime has its perils.

It is obvious to everyone, and has been reiterated countless times, that there is a *break* in Vigeland's artistic development. We can observe his struggle to get free of the intense, nervous style of his youth, and we can follow him as he works toward a more massive, powerful and monumental mode of expression. His figures grow rounder and fuller. This occurred sometime about 1910 to 1912. At the same time we find him striving for a harmoniousness which was lacking in the passionately conceived early works.

Within the utterly personal works of Vigeland's youth there is a flame burning with such intensity that he would surely have been consumed had he continued to give so much of himself to each work through a long productive life. He often claimed that for him, art was suffering and martyrdom. "The one person who has written most truly about me is Jens Thiis, who wrote that for me art was martyrdom."

Vigeland's impassioned nature had so much to convey to mankind that he could not take time to grapple with the problems inherent in the physical material itself. It is no easy matter to apply the stringent canons of esthetics to these moving early works. As the years passed however, and his stormy spirit grew calmer, the strength of his emotions was no longer so overwhelming. Ideas continued to pour out of his volcanic imagination; there was still no one who could match his capacity for plastic visualization; but the tenderness and sensitivity which had characterized a work like *Mother and Child* now gave way to the brute power of the later works, and his former humility turned to self-assured arrogance. Thus the formal shortcomings which were already noticeable in his early works became increasingly obvious.

Dedekam noted in 1922 that Vigeland was aware that the works of his youth "were sustained by their emotional strength, whereas their formal qualities in the light of his present standards, were far from perfect."

Vigeland returned constantly to the central problem of all creative artists — how to transpose emotion successfully into works of art. He claimed repeatedly that for him emotion was the prime factor and that it was a gift he had received when still in the cradle, but that mastery of form was something he

172

The Triangle, 1939—40.
Gustav Vigeland in 1918.

had had to struggle for. "Once," he said, "I thought it was enough to express emotion, a state of mind, without developing the formal aspects. Now I am of another opinion." He insisted that "There is as much sincerity in these recent studies as there was in my early works. But it is more concentrated. They are filled with the very same melancholy which I have been trying to escape from all my life."

As far back as 1902 he had written: *It is the transcendent in art which interests me. All the rest — drawing from models, painting from models, sculpting from models — they can keep as far as I am concerned, no matter how correct it all is . . .*

There is something in Gothic art which is so liberating. Though it is wooden in form, helpless even, yet it has feeling, and feeling is now the only thing which counts for me. Everything else is concocted, is estheticism, all this "how it ought to be." It affects me like lead weights hung on my arms and legs keeping me from getting anywhere. Although I want technique to matter as much as possible, I cannot bear it when art becomes artisanry, wrote Vigeland to Larpent in 1901. He frequently referred to the difficulty of keeping feeling alive in the finished work, as when he wrote to Larpent: *The worst thing of all is realizing how powerless one is to represent what one feels.* In 1930 he wrote to another friend: *Instead of increasing the distance between the work and one's feelings, making the way from the heart to the hand long, crooked and difficult by looking right and left and wondering how one person does it, how another has done it and how a third will do it — instead, one ought to work at shortening the distance; make it infinitely short. It cannot be short enough . . .* There are also later statements by Vigeland in a similar vein.

Gustav Vigeland belongs to that category of artists in whose works form cannot be separated from content. As he himself said: *The inner and outer aspects are born simultaneously; I have never had an idea which I have had to find a form for, nor have I had a visual concept which I have had to endow*

174

Detail from the group, Father and Daughter, p. 43.

with an idea. From the sketch to the finished work it is extremely rare for anything to be changed, apart from the demands imposed by a large work.

It is not something I strive for, no, it is natural for me to fuse instantaneously the two opposing elements — monumentality and emotion... I have tried to unite a monumental quality with feeling. My statues are always felt, and are not the result of reflection or calculation.

A few of Vigeland's statements about the actual process of creation have been preserved. Dedekam relates a conversation where Vigeland remarked: *The capacity for artistic creation was a gift, as it were, something sacred. The artist himself did not know where his ideas came from or how they occurred to him. The act of creation evaded every analysis and every thought-out explanation. Thus all great works of art speak to the passing generations, each generation interpreting them in its own way.*

In 1921 Vigeland remarked similarly to Aars: *I never had a choice; I was a sculptor before I was born. I was driven and*

175

lashed onwards by powerful forces outside myself. There was no other path, and no matter how hard I might have tried to find one I would have been forced back again. And again, half a year later: *I am convinced that there are strong forces outside us which we have no control over . . . We may be thinking of ordinary, everyday things when suddenly an idea appears, alive and complete, and there it is — something we had not thought about at all.* Or this: *An idea comes in two pauses between two sixteenths of a second.*

Speaking to Dedekam in 1921 about the unconscious and the unfathomable he had this to say: *It is divine. It is a gift. You get it for nothing. You are not master of it. It is not controlled by will. The imagination functions by itself. Creating works of art is no game, it is agony. All true artists are humble because they do not know when the gift will be taken away from them. It is the most tragic thing that can happen to an artist. Look at Michelangelo's bent figure and uncomely face: he is bowed beneath the burden of his divine gift and creates in agony. Genius escapes analysis.*

As for the connexion between the first-rate working conditions Vigeland was given and the decline in artistic quality which many people believe they can detect, one often hears this primitive reasoning: There you have it; when an artist is too comfortable his work gets poorer.

It is hardly that simple. Nevertheless if one day a study is made purposing to determine in what ways, both good and bad, Vigeland was affected by the contract, the results will surely prove interesting. In 1917, when he was still working in his ramshackle old studio, Vigeland made this note. *Now that the city is going to come and take the studio I am going to be forced out barefoot on the ice as it were. It cannot be otherwise when I am to be thrown out along with everything I have produced in the last 30 years. But there is no progress, no culture in this country. No, back to prehistoric times.*

176

The artist taking a lunch break in the little garden of his old studio, 1923.

To the ice-age. To the glaciers. To have your naked feet frozen fast there.

There is a note written eight years later, in 1925, indicating that in darker moments Vigeland may well have regretted signing the contract: *I would not have moved out if they had not wanted the site for something else and torn down my studio. I would have stayed there till the end of my days. I would not have traded all my original works, etc. for a building which was only a museum and not a studio. It was just when I lost my old studio that I needed a studio most of all.*

Not only did he refuse to sell his works to the city, but he would not accept a regular salary either: *I prefer not to be paid for my work. I cannot be like the girl who said, "Give me another shilling and I'll be passionate."*

177

Girl and a monster, 1938.
Erected in Frogner Park.
P. 179: The tree. Relief.
1905.

Vigeland could have been a rich man if he had been willing to sell his works, and if he had accepted all the offers which poured in from museums and collectors. However, he wanted everything he had made to remain together in his museum and in the Sculpture Park. For this reason there are only a few works by Vigeland to be found outside Norway, and nearly all of them are early works which he sold before making the agreement with the city.

Surely one of the unfortunate consequences of the contract was Vigeland's feeling that his works no longer belonged to him, and that henceforth he could not do what any artist ought to be able to do — go into his studio and appraise his works with a fresh eye, and perhaps even destroy the things which do not satisfy him. Vigeland instead began to save every sketch and every sentence he wrote, preserving even such worthless items as laundry bills and replies to classified advertisements. He kept absolutely everything, including the self-revelatory

jottings. The later Vigeland was a different man altogether from the youth who once said to his landlady, "You can keep my suitcase, but get rid of its contents for me." The contents were hundreds of drawings which were then emptied out on one of the hills outside Oslo and were scattered to the four winds. That time Vigeland really had felt free, for he had decided to begin again at the beginning. The later Vigeland, fettered by his contract, would never be able to feel that way again.

After signing the contract he set to work at a breath-taking pace. Prior to the contract he had had another period of intense productivity at the time when he expanded the plans for the Fountain. Yet he seems to have been simultaneously possessed by a feeling of impotency. Thus, in 1913, he wrote that whenever he was away from his studio he yearned to get back to it again. The night seemed endless. "When I get

179

to the studio I am powerless, paralysed." The period abounds in overly pessimistic remarks such as: *My time is past (1915). It seems that I look at everything through a haze. I feel dull, I walk in a trance, in a dream, half dead or, rather, as if I had died a great many years ago (1919).* It might be objected that such statements are merely sporadic depressions such as every person, and especially every artist, experiences from time to time. This may be so, but the outbursts occur with great frequency, and the pessimism they express is quite different from that of the early writings. They all follow the same trend, and they occur only in the private notebooks, seldom in letters. There is reason therefore to interpret them as the expression of a profound personal artistic crisis instead of a temporary depression. What is so remarkable is that this inner crisis coincides with a period of tremendous productivity.

Work was no longer the pure joy it had been. Statements such as "My work is devouring each hour of my life" (1913) were more and more frequent. It was as though he had begun a race against death. In a 1913 notebook one question appears repeatedly: "Will death come today?" Vigeland wrote the following, a first draught for a poem, in 1912:

I am a wandering tree
with loose roots.
A tree of trembling nerves,
with ever budding branches and twigs,
and leaves and buds fluttering
and quivering towards new agonies.

What buds are these
bursting forth from the tree of my spirit?
If I could stay the wild bud's blossoming
Oh, if I could thwart the growth of the wild buds
that I might grow in peace, quietly grow.
Toward heaven.

180

Woman and a monster. April 6—25, 1917.

Still the buds sprout on the tree of my life,
buds taking the sap,
sucking the marrow from the twigs and branches
which I know would endure — were
their nourishment not seized by the others.

"I stroked a dragon's head with the gentlest touch; by way of thanks it snapped at me." It is no coincidence that the dragon motif became more and more of an obsession. In 1912 in particular he made numerous sketches of dragons and humans in combat. There is even a drawing with a dragon clutching a man who has ceased to struggle, which Vigeland called a self-portrait.

When was that seed sown in my mind which now over-shadows my life? he cried in 1912.

When I was little I thought of carving all of mountainous Norway into one great figure. Now I am already old and I have only chipped at a couple of pebbles.

Vigeland retained his extraordinary powers of imagination and creativeness, but somehow his humility had left him. Now his works were born of spitefulness, of indignation and of wrath, and one colossal work after another took shape.

To take one example, Vigeland's lists for 1918 show that he made no less than ten large granite groups that year, including two of the tall dragon groups. In addition to these he made several studies and finished the cutting of his *Woman with Crossed Legs.*

Labouring under such a tremendous amount of self-imposed work, it was no wonder that Vigeland withdrew more and more from the outside world. Yet he could write of his isolation with a certain droll humour, as in this excerpt from 1934: *One day I went out into the street and all the women had pulled their skirts up to their knees. I thought I was in a madhouse, a city of crazy people, and I could hardly believe my eyes. It was only that fashions had changed since the last*

Smoking on the sea-side rocks.   Resting on the grass.

Chatting with a farmer.

time I had been out. The next time I went out all the skirts were down again.

He told his friend Aars in 1922: *If I have only been out of the studio for a little while, just for a breath of air, I feel like a stranger when I come in again. I find myself estranged from my work. The day is spoiled; it is as though something had shattered inside me.*

Even though Gustav Vigeland led a secluded life in his studio, his notes and his extensive library show that he kept abreast of events, and that he read a great deal — literature as well as treatises on art. On several occasions he told his friends that he wished he could have been like other people and "capture joy."

His collaborators, who both admired and feared him, knew him as more than the reserved and distant artist. They saw his generosity, his droll wit and humor.

Every summer he left his studio to spend a few weeks at his summer cottage, "Breime," near Lindesnes at the southern tip of Norway. There, together with his young wife Ingerid and his little "holiday child" Kari, he felt free and happy in the company of a few close friends. It was then he could "capture joy." In periods of happiness he would sometimes exclaim to his friend Dedekam, "My soul is as peaceful as a calm sea."

Back in the studio however, there awaited him the overwhelming tasks which he had imposed upon himself. Viewed from the vantage point of the present we can see now what a great strain the hectic creative efforts of Vigeland's race against death must have been. Early in his career he had stated that art was martyrdom for him. He bore this martyrdom knowingly, though feeling that he was under the dictates of a power outside himself. A human condition such as this is not the easiest foundation for creative work. In certain cases it can lead to diminished objectivity in the artist's evaluation of his own work, especially when he feels

184

Drawing for "The Damned," dated Nov. 5, 1897.

forced into such great productivity. It is this which, in the final account, was the aging master's unresolvable dilemma.

Vigeland was well aware that having lost his youth, he had lost with it certain qualities which had infused and carried his early works. Nor, in his candid moments, did he attempt to conceal it. He knew that the works of his youth had their weaknesses, primarily of a formal nature, and he attempted therefore to advance along another path. However, the simple fact that there was so much he felt he *had* to do may have resulted in his not always having the necessary time and energy to work out solutions to the problems of form which occupied him.

Gustav Vigeland fought his battle, contending with his artistic and personal problems, and though he was by no means a poet he turned, in difficult moments, to the medium of poetry to give vent to his feelings and to the recognition of his situation as a man and as an artist. In fact the term artist in its usual sense is hardly applicable to him — sculptor, rather.

"I was a sculptor before I was born," he had said of himself.

In 1935 when Gustav Vigeland was 66, he took a poem which he had written during his artistic crisis in 1912, reworked it and wrote it down in its final form. It is the sculptor's poetic "autobiography."

> When I was young I stormed at life
> attacking it as though it were an enemy.
> I did not listen to its voice
> but tore at it with beak and savage claws.
>
> From this came figures, linear, spare, gaunt,
> so like the self I was, so bony, sinewy,
> a tautness which I fashioned in ecstasy,
> yet thought came too late for my idea.
>
> Upon that time it seems, my breath came audibly
> more out than in and with an ardent groan.
> But now the storm alone can fill my lungs —
> I breathe as it were, more in than out.
>
> Because my life toils towards equipoise,
> and I respire but halfway in my works,
> I wish the heart would forcibly enjoin
> that both breathing motions be of equal strength.

The Oslo Philharmonic, conducted by Øivind Fjeldstad.
The free summer concerts which the city of Oslo sponsors in the courtyard
of the Vigeland Museum are very popular.

SOME IMPORTANT DATES

1869   born in Mandal.

1884   learns wood-carving in Oslo.

1886   father dies.

1889   studies at the School of Drawing and with Brynjulf Bergslien, later with Mathias Skeibrok.

1889   makes debut at State Art Exhibition with group, Hagar and Ishmael.

1891   goes to Copenhagen on state stipend, studies under Prof. Bissen for one year.

1891   The Accursed.

1892   Young Girl.

1892   goes to Paris at age of 23, is greatly impressed by Rodin's works.

1893   Hell I.

1893   Consolation.

1894   first independent exhibition.

1895   travels to Berlin and Florence.

1896   revisits Italy. Florence – Rome – Naples.

1897   Hell II.

1897 – 1907 works on restauration of Trondheim cathedral.

1899   second independent exhibition.

1900   marries Laura Mathilde Andersen.

1900 – 1901 travels in France and England to study Gothic art.

1902   moves into studio in Hammersborg part of Oslo.

1905   Monument to Niels Henrik Abel (erected 1908).

1905   Rikard Nordraak commemorative statue (erected 1911).

1905   Man Holding Woman in his Arms.

1906   first version of the Fountain, intended for Studenterlund Gardens.

1906   Man and Woman (marble).

1906   statue of Ludwig van Beethoven.

1907   mother dies.

1907   Henrik Wergeland commemorative statue (erected 1908).

1907   Mother and Child.

1907   the first Vigeland-committee formed to raise money for Fountain.

1908   the Hammersborg studio enlarged.

1908   The Beggars.

1909   Camilla Collett commemorative statue (erected 1911).

1909   Torso of a Woman.

1914   Vigeland plans to place Fountain-complex on Abel Hill.

1916   the Hammersborg studio open to the public.

189

1916   Commemorative statue of Tordenskiold, the Norwegian naval hero.
1917   a new Vigeland-committee to finance the granite groups.
1917   woodcut exhibition at the Kunstnerforbundet's gallery.
1920   Girl on a Reindeer.
1921   contract with the city signed.
1921   Girl on a Bear.
1922   marries Ingerid Vilberg.
1922   self-portrait.
1923   Egil Skallagrimsson.
1923   moves into new studio designed by architect Lorentz Ree.
1924 – 25 models Column with 122 figures - «The Monolith».
1929   decorated with Great Cross of St. Olav.
1930   opens studio to public.
1931   City Council approves plans for Sculpture Park.
1933 – 34 Wheel of Life.
1943   dies at Lovisenberg Hospital, Oslo.
1947   Vigeland Museum is opened in what was formerly the artist's studio.

OTHER BOOKS ON GUSTAV VIGELAND IN ENGLISH

There are a number of books which have been published in Norwegian on Gustav Vigeland. Some of them are also available in English.

Ragna Stang: Gustav Vigeland 1869–1969. Tanum 1969.
(Also available in German).

Ragna Stang: The Vigeland Sculpture Park in Oslo. Tanum 1970.
(Also available in German and French).

Gustav Vigeland. The condition of Man.
Illustrated catalogue with several articles. Vigeland-museet 1976.
(Available only from the Vigland Museum).